HOW MY MIND HAS CHANGED

How My Mind
Has Changed

Essays from the
Christian Century

Edited by
DAVID HEIM

CASCADE *Books* · Eugene, Oregon

HOW MY MIND HAS CHANGED
Essays from the *Christian Century*

Cascade Books
An Imprint of Wipf and Stock Publishers
199 W. 8th Ave., Suite 3
Eugene, OR 97401

www.wipfandstock.com

ISBN 13: 978-1-62032-478-3

The poem by Micheal O'Siadhail originally appeared in *The Chosen Garden* (Dedalus Press, 1990) and subsequently in *Poems 1975–1995* (Bloodaxe, 1999). Used by permission of Bloodaxe Books.

Cataloging-in-Publication data:

How my mind has changed : essays from the *Christian Century* / edited by David Heim.

viii + 124 p. ; 23 cm.

ISBN 13: 978-1-62032-478-3

1. Theology. 2. Theology—History—20th century. 3. Theology—History—21st century. I. Heim, David. II. Title.

BR85 .H49 2012

Manufactured in the U.S.A.

Contents

Preface

IN 1939 THE EDITORS of the *Christian Century* asked a group of theologians to reflect on "how my mind has changed in this decade." It seemed apparent that the 1930s were a pivotal decade, an unavoidable challenge to intellectual complacency. The editors had in mind the major events of the era—the Great Depression, the rise of fascism in Europe, the signs of another world war on the horizon. They were also mindful that a new era had already arisen in theology: "neo-orthodoxy," whether that of Karl Barth or of Reinhold Niebuhr, had issued a formidable challenge to liberal theology. The editors thought that the new situation demanded a response. They asked theologians to give their individual testimony and published the resulting essays as a series.

Testimony means personal witness—stating what you can't but believe is true. Theology always involves testimony of some kind, since its subject cannot be a matter of disinterested inquiry. One is either passionately interested in God or it is not God that one is interested in. As Luther put it: "It is by living—no, much more still by dying—that one becomes a theologian, not by knowing, reading, or speculation."

The essays in this book make up the sixth installment of the series How My Mind Has Changed. The *Century's* editors cited Luther's words in inviting theologians to reflect on their own passions, struggles, and hopes as people of faith. We asked them to consider how their work and life have been intertwined. Unlike the editors of the 1930s, we did not suppose that changes of mind could be defined by or traced to a single decade. But we did urge writers to consider what events or experiences—personal, public, and professional—had shaped their theological commitments or inspired some second thoughts.

Contemporary events—the culture war in the United States, struggles for justice at home and abroad, global encounters with ethnic and religious diversity, experiences of exclusion and oppression—play a role in many of these stories, sometimes a decisive one. In other cases, political and cultural contentions are the backdrop to a journey shaped primarily by personal relationships and personal challenges within the academic study of theology.

These essays display the renewed energy that theology has found in the postmodern context. No longer constrained by a narrow Enlightenment model of what constitutes rationality, theologians have been freed to use first-order religious language and to make constructive theological claims. They have been able to explore—to cite examples from this collection—the reasoning embodied in a textual tradition and the deep wisdom embodied in practices of worship, prayer, and community solidarity.

Moreover, it appears from these essays that the always rough distinction between "liberal" and "postliberal" theologies is increasingly passé. A deep commitment to the church and to the creedal and biblical tradition by no means precludes an extensive use of the social sciences or tools used by religious studies. Indeed, a renewed confidence in theology as a comprehensive discipline seems to invite, perhaps demand, just such an engagement.

Giving religious testimony means talking less about how you have grasped God and more about how God has grasped you. In providing such a testimony, these writers offer a unique window on their thoughts and endeavors, the theological scene, and the varied and unsuspected ways that God is at work.

These essays appeared in the pages of the *Christian Century* during 2009, 2010, and 2011. Thanks to the *Century* editorial staff—John Buchanan, Richard Kauffman, Debra Bendis, Steve Thorngate, Amy Frykholm, and Dean Peerman—for helping produce the series, and special thanks to Siobhan Drummond for copyediting all the essays and preparing this collection.

David Heim

1

Turning Points

PAUL J. GRIFFITHS

CHANGES OF MIND AREN'T superficial or easy things. Mine have usually come as forced exits from the comfort of myself to somewhere more painful. I have had to learn to be beside myself.

In the late autumn of 1976, in the ground-floor reading room of the University of Oxford's New Bodleian Library, I decide that I need to be baptized. I'm twenty. It's a sunny day, I've just had my morning coffee in the King's Arms across the street, and I've been reading Athanasius in preparation for a tutorial on the Arian heresy. The tableau—the sun across the blond wood reading tables, the soft smells of damp wool and old paper, the feel of sandals on my feet as I walk up and down beside the tall stacks of shelves—is clear to me still. Baptism is one decision among several: I also decide which languages I need to learn to read, or to read better (French, German, Latin, Greek), and which thinkers I need more intimate acquaintance with (Augustine, Heidegger, Wittgenstein).

I go, a few days later, to speak with my college chaplain, Trevor Williams, about being baptized. He treats me with kindness and undertakes to instruct me in preparation for baptism the following Easter. He is Anglican, and so I am baptized into the Anglican Communion. I consider no other. I am English, after all, and this is Oxford. I am hazily aware that there are other churches, other communions; but I give almost no consideration to their differences, and likewise none to Anglican specificities. I think, with some justice, that I already know more theology than most Anglicans and that what I need is simply the sacrament. Six months later or so, at Easter in 1977 at the church of Saint Mary Magdalene in Oxford, I am baptized and subsequently become a regular communicant and occasional petitioner of God for this and that.

I was then—it seems to me now, more than three decades later—as profoundly self-centered as most people of that age. And the reception of the sacraments had no transformative effect upon the fabric of my experience or upon my intellectual passions—none, at least, then discernible to me. I would not have wanted them to. But in fact, I now think, the reception of the sacraments was efficacious: it began gradually to set me aside, to place me beside myself, and, equally slowly, to make of my studies less an instrument for self-gratification and the domination of others and more an ecstasy of response to God.

Five years after my baptism, in the late spring of 1982 on a cold, bright day by Lake Mendota in Madison, Wisconsin, I find myself again beside myself, this time with anger and frustration. I am twenty-six. I have been for some time studying Indian Buddhist thought and am at the moment receiving instruction from Geshe Lhundup Sopa in the technicalities of Buddhist metaphysics. He is a monk and a scholastic, then perhaps in his fifties, trained in the systematic thought of the Tibetan Gelug school. He is teaching a graduate seminar at the University of Wisconsin in Madison, where I am a student in a doctoral program in Buddhist studies. He is my adviser and has been teaching me for close on a year, especially in the *Abhidhar-makosa*, a fourth-century Sanskritic summa of Buddhist thought; but I am angry with his teaching methods and with him and want to find a way out.

There is a long distance between Oxford and Madison and, in a different way, between the study of theology in the former place and that of Buddhist metaphysics in the latter. I have traversed those distances theologically. My Oxford studies and my baptism have raised for me the theological question of what Christians should think and teach about long-lived traditions of religious thought and practice other than their own. I had decided, with the absurd confidence of youth and still as an Oxford undergraduate, that I would answer this question, and that in order to do so I must gain substantive expertise in an alien tradition by learning to speak it as a second first language—to handle its lexicon and syntax as if I were a native speaker. I chose, for local and contingent reasons, to do this with

Indian Buddhism, which involves the study of Sanskrit and, eventually, Tibetan, and after beginning those studies at Oxford I moved to Wisconsin to pursue them in greater depth. That is what has led me to the study of the *Abhidharmakosa* under the tutelage of Geshe Sopa.

Sopa teaches as a scholastic and as one thoroughly textualized. He has memorized the texts from which he teaches—the Tibetans like to say that if you have your learning in a book on the shelf at home, then of course you don't really have it; it needs to be in your head, ready to go—and he teaches and thinks in deep conversation with his texts. Each class begins with a chant of the verses memorized for that day and proceeds to oral exposition of the text. Sopa has no interest in the questions that concern me—questions about textual transmission, about versions, about whether there are good reasons to think that the central claims of the texts he expounds are true, and about the relations between Buddhism and Christianity; he simply teaches, calmly. If he does not find a question interesting or thinks it irrelevant to the matter at hand, he smiles and nods and leaves it aside by returning to the text. He embodies his text and gives voice to it.

I want other things. I want to be given the skills that will provide me an academic career. I want my questions answered. I want him to argue with me. I do not want to submit to his text, and certainly not to him. My anger is about all those things. I vent it, take another adviser, finish my work with dispatch—a six-hundred-page dissertation on Indian Buddhist meditation theory, arduously typed and retyped—find a job at the University of Chicago and begin, with rapidity and ambition, to claw my way up the academic ladder.

Geshe Sopa placed me beside myself with anger. He also showed me, though I was not then remotely ready to see it, what it might be like to set oneself aside in favor of a textual tradition, to permit oneself to be overwritten by it and made its creature. His lessons in this I can now see for what they were, and I am grateful for them. I learned from him what I had not learned from my Christian teachers, which is how to read. It took me a decade or so to begin to make sense of the lesson and to begin to use it as a reader of the Christian text. That is a practice in which I am still engaged and will be until death and beyond.

Spring at the University of Notre Dame in Indiana is a gorgeous time: the campus is especially beautiful. Mary, golden atop the dome that can be seen from almost everywhere on campus, smiles, and the world is as it should be. But in the spring of 1988, five years after I've received my doctorate, I find myself angry once again, angry enough that I am ready to resign from an academic career then in its early stages. I am thirty-two. The occasion for this anger is a seminar I have recently attended, given by a colleague from the anthropology department (I am teaching in theology) on the subject of Christian-Muslim relations. I have raised with him the question of whether, in his view, it is ever appropriate to argue with Muslims about the adequacy of their understanding of God in light of Christian trinitarian conviction. He replies, calmly and reasonably, that this is never appropriate, that we are surely past that outdated and harmful emphasis on apologetics and mission. Isn't understanding what we need to seek?

I argue, too polemically and too angrily and without subtlety, that he is selling the idea of truth short and that being a Christian means, among other things, having deep convictions about the crucial significance of Jesus Christ for the entire cosmos and thus understanding the Christian narrative as capable of embracing all others just as Christ was eager to embrace everyone, Muslims included. I convince him of nothing and spend the next few days stewing over the event.

It gradually assumes symbolic significance for me. I come to see it as representative of all that is bad about the academic life. If what the academy does to Christians is make them incapable of seeing the importance of the gospel's truth, then why am I in it? Am I not a Christian? Am I not supposed to be preaching the gospel? How can I bear to spend a career immured in this hell? I convince myself that I can't. After several days of discussion with long-suffering faculty colleagues—Joseph Wawrykow acts a saintly part here—and an even longer suffering and supportive spouse, I decide to resign my position effective at the end of the academic year and write a letter formally saying so to my chair and dean. That dean, Nathan Hatch, now president of Wake Forest University, is humane and perceptive. He tells me that he will sit on my resignation letter for six weeks, and if at the end of that time I still want to resign, he will accept it. If not, he will tear it up.

For the next few weeks I am, again, beside myself. There is, I am sure, something importantly right in my judgments about the academic enterprise; but it is equally obvious to me that there is something wrong with the passion and vehemence with which my own sense of being right is suffused. I become increasingly aware, too, that I have real and nonnegotiable practical responsibilities to my wife and two small children (then one and four years old). I back down and withdraw my resignation and am graciously received back into the academic community at Notre Dame—much more graciously than I deserve.

I was learning something. The most important thing, I now think, was the lesson that, yes, Jesus does trump the university, and that, yes, my primary loyalty is to him. I had, for the previous five years, been trying hard to forget Geshe Sopa's lessons in reading and to dry out my baptismal soaking of eleven years before in the harsh fires of academic ambition. What Augustine likes to call the *libido dominandi* had assumed an excessive importance: I had published my first book; a second was on the way; I was publishing essays and articles; and I had my eye on early tenure. Everything was in place, but my affections—my loves—were misweighted and that out-of-jointness was in part corrected, or at least moved in the direction of correction, by this incident.

This lesson began to bear fruit in ways that even I could see. I found a renewed delight in my sacramental life as an Episcopalian; I sought my local bishop's permission to preach, which he gave, and for a number of years I preached, off and on, in pulpits in the Episcopal Diocese of Northern Indiana; and I began to write more explicitly theological work, combining my historical and exegetical work on Buddhism with Christian theological analyses of and responses to that tradition and writing some books and essays on how Christians should respond to the facts of religious diversity. I began to read widely and with passion in contemporary theology—George Lindbeck and Alasdair MacIntyre were important here, as later was John Milbank; I discovered Hans Urs von Balthasar; I read the early encyclicals of John Paul II and as a result began to read almost everything that appeared above his name. These men, of course, do not agree about everything; what I liked in them was the primacy that each of them gave to the Christian claim and the intellectual confidence with which they expounded that primacy.

Anger is, among the seven deadly sins, the most ambiguous. It is the least clearly sinful and the most possibly fruitful. For me, it has often accompanied the ecstasy of being drawn away from myself, set beside myself and thereby closer to God.

Independence Day 1996, in Chennai (once Madras), South India. A hot day, like all July days there. The sweat runs between my shoulder blades as I pace the roof. I am forty. I am spending the summer in a Jesuit-run ashram called Aikiya Alayam, on the edge of the city. I am teaching now at the University of Chicago Divinity School and working on a book called *Religious Reading: The Place of Reading in the Practice of Religion.* I am in India to read and write, and for a breathing space. The work is going well, and I can see the shape of the book before me. I am Anglican still: I am going to the nearest congregation of the Church of South India on Sundays and attending daily mass with the Jesuits during the week. After a week or so and some considerable conferring among themselves, they invite me to participate fully in their daily mass, and I happily do so. I've not much notion of the doctrine and discipline of the Catholic Church on these matters and so am not fully sensible of the complexities of this position. I am, however, grateful for the hospitality shown me.

The sisters who prepare food and run the place had surprised me the week before by bringing me a special cake on the 29th of June. They assumed that I would know why, but I don't. They laughed, and although we have little language in common, they eventually got it across to me that this day is the Solemnity of Peter and Paul and therefore my name day, my saint's day, a proper occasion for celebration. They know that I am not Catholic, and I think they were amused by the depth of my Protestant ignorance about things that matter. I was moved almost to tears by the unexpectedness of the gesture and by the vistas opened to me by it: a world in which the communion of saints is an everyday matter. This was the beginning of another derailment, another progressive setting aside of myself.

It deepens a few days later. I'm walking past the Catholic Cathedral in Chennai, pondering whether to go in, when a large crowd of people makes a noisy exit. They gather behind a decrepit but beribboned and garlanded flatbed truck, and as it moves slowly away, they walk behind it, singing. More and more people join them as the truck makes a slow pilgrimage through the city. Bad (to my ear) and very loud recorded music blares from speakers on the truck. People begin to dance and sing. I follow, wondering what is going on. I manage to ask and to understand some part of the answers given me. I learn that an image of Saint Thomas the Apostle is being paraded through the city as part of the celebration of that saint's feast day on July 3. I have long known that Thomas was supposed to have brought Christianity to India, and this piece of knowledge now comes alive. I learn that his relics are enshrined in the cathedral and that there is great local devotion to him. By now there are thousands of people following the truck-borne image, and I, along with them, am transported.

The next day, Independence Day, I walk the roof of the ashram in the heat of the afternoon (mad dogs and Englishmen: everyone else is sleeping), restless and still ecstatic. I contrast the deep and direct devotional passions I've seen the day before with the staid and oddly English worship I've been experiencing in the Church of South India. I think of the Jesuits and their mass, celebrated early in the morning with the cool breeze blowing through the portico, the sweet smells of flowering trees whose names I do not know, and the soft mixture of Tamil and Latin caressing my ears. I meditate upon the sisters who knew my name day when I did not and gave me the ability to celebrate it. I think of John Paul II's witness and work.

It is suddenly and strikingly obvious that I should seek full unity with the bishop of Rome. I've long known that there are no theological or other conceptual difficulties for me in that move; and I have occasionally toyed with the thought of what it would be like to be Catholic. But it had remained a thought, and now it is a conviction. Five months later, on the third Sunday of Advent in 1996, I am received into the Catholic Church at the parish church of Saint Thomas Apostle on the South Side of Chicago.

It's a bright, cool day in Durham, North Carolina. I'm fifty-three. I'm writing the account you are reading not in an ecstasy of self-forgetfulness and not in anger, but with some puzzlement at the difficulty of doing such a thing. I've written it in vignettes rather than as a connected, sequential account because that is how it appears to me. I am deeply opaque to myself in the present and even more so as the present recedes into the past. My Oxford self of 1976 is almost completely gone, and my later selves in Wisconsin, Notre Dame, and Chennai are not much more available. What stands out, in bright relief, are tableaus: short sequences of events whose details are vivid and whose power remains strong. But the connections that would string those vignettes into a narrative are mostly dark; to supply them would require an act of imagination at present beyond me and were I to attempt it now the result would be a fiction, a figment, a phantasm.

What remains is gratitude for the God-given gift of time, of thought, and of the companionship of the saints, living and dead. Two among the dead—John Henry Newman and Aurelius Augustinus—have been my constant companions since even before my Oxford days. They showed me, before I had any hope of understanding it (I still have not much), the scope and flexibility and fascination of the gospel's challenge to thought. An ever-present thread in my intellectual life (how hard it is to use that phrase without pomposity) has been this sense, inchoate and undeveloped, of gratitude for the gift of tools with which to think. My Anglican teachers gave me Christian language and a first acquaintance with the work of those who had used it before me. My Buddhist teachers showed me what it is to submit, joyfully and with intellectual energy, to a tradition of thought and practice and how, therefore, to read.

And my more than twelve years in the warmly embracing arms of the Catholic Church have given me the whole of the tradition, a vastly expanded range of authorities and teachers with whom to think, and a cloud of witnesses, living and dead, to chide me and support me and take me further from this burdensome self, whose spectacular inner theater it is the business of Christians gradually to transform into an outer-directed voice, a small note in the chorus of praise to the God who is not a being among beings, but rather the giver of being itself. As Augustine writes: *non solum non peccemus adorando, sed peccemus non adorando*, which is to say that adoration of God is both necessary and sufficient for the avoidance of sin. I have not changed my mind about that, but I have come to see its meaning more clearly.

2

The Way to Justice

NICHOLAS WOLTERSTORFF

AUTOBIOGRAPHY DOES NOT COME easy to me. I grew up in a community of Dutch Reformed immigrants in a tiny farming village in southwest Minnesota. The ethos of the Dutch Reformed was never to call attention to oneself, to be modest in all things, never to brag or boast, never to toot your own horn. If you have done something well, let others say so; don't say it yourself. The Minnesota ethos was always to understate. If someone compliments you for some fine job you have done, either say "Thanks" and let it go at that or say, "Yah, not bad, I suppose." If a fellow student asks how you did on your report card and you got all As, say "Done worse." Of course, lying is out. So if you have never done worse, if you have always gotten all As, say "Seen worse." Autobiography feels awkward, self-conscious, indecent, rather like exposing oneself in public. But I will do my best.

That immigrant Dutch Reformed community in which I grew up was poor. Its poverty was not grinding poverty, but almost all families were poor. And it was egalitarian; people were treated alike. Had there been any wealth to be ostentatiously displayed, the community would have firmly disapproved of such display. Much later I learned about Max Weber's thesis that the origins of capitalism are to be found in the ethos of early Calvinism; the Calvinists, so said Weber, regarded financial success as a sign of God's favor. The attitude of my father was the exact opposite. He automatically assumed that if someone in the community was beginning to accumulate substantial wealth, that was not to be attributed to God's favor but to shady dealing.

Behind Weber's interpretation of early Calvinism was his belief that "double predestination" was prominent in its ethos; financial success was regarded as the sign that one was numbered among the elect, so Weber thought. I dare say that double predestination was prominent in the Dutch Reformed ethos of the seventeenth century. But I myself don't recall ever hearing it preached or taught. It was something that we young people pestered our ministers about in catechism classes. The ministers all seemed uncomfortable and defensive when the topic came up; this encouraged us to press on in pestering them. The image of God that I picked up was not the image of an arbitrary tyrant but an image of majesty and awesomeness.

If double predestination was not prominent in the version of Calvinism in which I was reared, what was? If asked as a teenager, I would probably have spouted some folklore about what differentiated us from the German Catholics and Norwegian Lutherans surrounding us there in Minnesota—and from the Presbyterians in our town whom we called "Americans." It was not until I was a student at Calvin College in Grand Rapids, Michigan, that I came to self-understanding.

Doctrine and theological discussion have always been prominent in the Dutch Reformed tradition. But the professors who inspired me at Calvin College were not theologians. Though they were very good at discussing theology when the occasion arose, they did not spout doctrine. They had imbibed the mentality and spirituality of Abraham Kuyper, the Dutch theologian and activist of the last three decades of the nineteenth century and the first two of the twentieth; what they instilled in us, their students, was Kuyper's neo-Calvinism.

If I had to put into as few words as possible what that mentality and spirituality were, it would go something like this: God's call to those who are Christ's followers is to participate in the life of the church and to think, feel, speak, and act as Christians within the institutions and practices that we share with our fellow human beings. We are not called to go off by ourselves somewhere to set up our own economic practices, our own political institutions, our own art world, our own world of scholarship; we are called to participate within our shared human practices and institutions.

But we are not to participate within these practices and institutions like everybody else, then adding on our Christian faith. Christian faith is not an add-on. There is no religiously and morally neutral way of participating in these practices and institutions. Everybody participates as *who they are*; and whatever else each of us may be, we are creatures who have convictions about God and the world, about life, about the good and the right. These convictions shape, in subtle and not so subtle ways, what we do when we participate in those shared practices and institutions.

To this must be added the obvious fact that there is no consensus among human beings on these matters; we disagree on matters of religion and morality, we sometimes disagree, sometimes profoundly, in our comprehensive perspectives. Thus it is that the Christian participates, or should participate, qua Christian, just as the naturalist participates qua naturalist and the humanist qua humanist. The practices and institutions are shared, but the way in which we participate in them is not neutral but pluralist.

That was the vision that we as students at Calvin College in the 1950s were taught. When it came to the life of the Christian in scholarship, the vision was encapsulated in the Augustinian-Anselmian formula, "Faith seeking understanding." Not faith added to understanding, but faith seeking understanding. What Augustine and Anselm meant by the formula is that the Christian scholar is called to transmute what he already accepts on faith into something that he now knows and no longer merely believes. What our teachers meant by the formula was that the Christian scholar is called to participate in the academic discipline of, say, psychology in such a way that she sees through the eyes of faith the reality that the psychologist studies. This does not mean that everything there looks different to her from how it looks to those who are not Christian. Enough that *some* things look different.

This is a far cry from the habit, common among Christian academics, of developing theologies of this and of that—a theology of psychology, for example, or of aesthetics. A theology of aesthetics is *about* aesthetics; it is meta-aesthetics. That's different from looking at aesthetic reality through the eyes of faith.

Note that nothing has been said about constructing proofs for God's existence, about collecting evidence for the reliability of Christian scripture, and so forth. Our teachers had no interest whatsoever in evidentialism: no interest in evidence, more evidence, yet more evidence. It's not that they explicitly opposed evidentialism; they simply showed no interest in it. They took for granted that one did not have to have proofs and carefully assembled evidence to be entitled to be Christian. I took a course in which we worked through the first twenty or so "questions" in Aquinas's *Summa theologiae*. We studied Aquinas's "five ways" in depth and at length. Never did our teacher suggest that our Christian faith did or should hang on one or another proof for God's existence turning out to be both sound and persuasive to all rational human beings.

This "Kuyperian" vision which I imbibed in college has remained mine throughout my life. I have tried in some of my writings to articulate the vision itself in far more detail than my college teachers ever did; recent developments in philosophical epistemology have been of great aid in that. And I have been pushed, nudged, and jolted to work out the vision in directions that I was not at the time inclined toward. My life in scholarship has been the opposite of the classic German professor—I caricature—who at the age of twenty-five has a vision for a fifteen-volume system and hopes that his death will roughly coincide with the completion of the final volume. But the vision itself has remained steady—no reversals, no conversions, no dramatic changes of mind.

And it has stood me in good stead over the years. It helped me when I bumped up against logical positivism in my graduate philosophy studies at Harvard. A central part of the positivist position was that every attempt to say anything about God is without meaning. Since my faith was not based on proofs, I did not find myself worried that this contention of the positivists had undermined the proofs. Instead I found myself standing back with something like calm bemusement. I discerned that the deep-lying conviction that led the positivists to say what they were saying was that modern natural science is the only road to human progress. I found this totally implausible. Thus not for a moment did I believe that the positivists had uncovered the objective truth of the matter and that I either had to give up my Christian faith or figure out how to accommodate it to the truth now once and for all delivered by the positivists. I have always found jumping on and off academic bandwagons—all too common among my fellow Christians in the academy—to be unseemly, even disgusting.

Now for some of the pushes, nudges, and jolts. After finishing grad school, I taught for two years in the philosophy department at Yale. I then returned to my alma mater, Calvin College, to teach in the philosophy department (which I did for thirty years before returning to Yale). In September 1976 Calvin sent me to participate in a conference at the University of Potchefstroom in South Africa. Potchefstroom is not far from Johannesburg; the university at the time was run by the Doppers, a theologically conservative version of the Dutch Reformed tradition in South Africa. There were quite a few Dutch scholars present at the conference, a few of us from Canada and the United States, both blacks and whites from other parts of Africa, and Afrikaners from South Africa along with blacks and so-called coloreds.

The Dutch were very angry at the Afrikaners over apartheid and very knowledgeable about it, so they exploited every opening they could find to express their anger. The Afrikaners were very angry at the Dutch for being so angry at them and exploited every opening they could find to say so. After about a day and a half of this angry back-and-forth, neither party had anything new to say. It was then that the blacks and coloreds from South Africa began to speak up, more quietly than the Dutch and the Afrikaners. They spoke movingly of the ways in which they were daily humiliated and demeaned, they described what the apartheid system was doing to their people, and they cried out for justice.

The response of the Afrikaners took me completely aback. They did not contest the claim of the blacks and coloreds that they were being treated unjustly. Instead they insisted that justice was not a relevant category. The relevant category was love, charity, benevolence. They proceeded to tell stories about the ways in which they exhibited charity toward blacks and coloreds. They gave Christmas gifts to the blacks living in their backyards, passed on used clothing to the children, and so on. And they argued that it was not self-interest but benevolence that motivated the entire system of apartheid. The overall aim was to allow the eleven or so different nations (peoples) in South Africa each to find its own identity. That would be impossible if they were all mixed through each other; they had to be separated. That was the grand goal of apartheid. The Afrikaners concluded by saying that they felt hurt that blacks and coloreds so seldom expressed gratitude for the charity extended to them. Turning to the blacks and coloreds in the conference, they pleaded, "Why can't we just be brothers in Christ and love each other?"

Scales fell off my eyes. What I saw, as I had never seen before, was benevolence being used as an instrument of oppression. I felt called by God, in the classic Protestant sense of *call*, to speak up for these wronged and suffering people and to speak up for justice.

A year and a half later, in May 1978, I attended a conference on Palestinian rights on the West Side of Chicago. I never learned why I was invited, and I have never understood what it was in myself that led me to attend. But I did. There were about 150 Palestinians present, and they emphatically identified themselves as Palestinians, not as Arabs who just happened to live in Palestine. Most of them were Christian. They poured out their guts in flaming rhetoric—rhetoric too hot, I subsequently learned, for most Americans to handle. They too spoke of the ways in which they were daily demeaned; they spoke of how they had been dispossessed of their land in 1948 and of how that dispossession was continuing. And they too issued a call for justice. Again I felt that I had been called by God to speak up for these wronged and suffering people and to speak up for justice.

I have tried on a few occasions to put into words why it was that I was so moved by this cry for justice coming from South Africa and from the Palestinians. I had opposed the Vietnam War. But I had not been affected in the same way by it, and I had not thought much in terms of justice. Let me here forego any attempt at self-understanding and just say that being confronted by a call from God to speak up for these and other wronged people and to speak up for justice has profoundly shaped my subsequent life. I have spoken up in opposition to apartheid; I have spoken up for the Palestinians. And the topic of justice has become more prominent than any other in my writing. In 1983 I published *Until Justice and Peace Embrace*; in 2008 I published *Justice: Rights and Wrongs*. I am presently bringing to completion a manuscript on the relation between love and justice that I am tentatively calling *Justice in Love* (2011).

Handed down to us from antiquity are two comprehensive impera-tives. One, coming to us from both Greco-Roman antiquity and Jewish-Christian antiquity, is the imperative to do justice; the other, coming to us only from Jewish-Christian antiquity, is the imperative to love one's neigh-bor as oneself. On the face of it, these two imperatives do not display how they are related. Hence it is that the topic of the relation between love and justice pervades the literature of the West. Prominent in discussions of the topic is the theme of tension. Love sometimes does injustice, or appears to do so; justice is sometimes unloving, or appears to be so.

From the time I first began speaking and writing about justice, I have encountered this theme of tension in the response of my fellow Christians. Not in all of them, of course, but in many. Almost invariably it's because they have learned to interpret the New Testament as saying that in the teaching and life of Jesus, love has supplanted justice. Justice is outmoded Old Testament stuff. When I explain how I think of justice, the resistance becomes even more pronounced. I think of justice as grounded in the hon-oring of rights; a society is just insofar as the rights of its members, and of the society itself, are honored. A society is just insofar as no one is wronged. I remember a dear friend standing up in the question period after a talk I had given on justice and saying, with quavering voice, "Nick, nobody has any rights; it's grace all the way down!"

In *Justice in Love*, I wrestle with this theme of tension between love and justice, and with the interpretation of the New Testament which holds that in it love supplants justice. Malformed love does indeed come into conflict with justice. But well-formed love incorporates doing justice; justice is the ground floor of well-formed love. To delete justice from the Bible is to have very little left; that holds for the New Testament as well as the Old.

And as to the claim one often hears—that the idea of rights is alien to Christianity, that the idea was invented by secular thinkers of the Enlightenment and carries possessive individualism in its DNA—I say, to the contrary, that recent scholarship makes it indisputably clear that the idea of natural rights was explicitly and prolifically employed by the canon lawyers of the 1100s and again by leaders in the early Reformed tradition. Rights are what respect for worth requires; and in the opening chapter of Genesis we learn that God created us as creatures of great worth. The idea of human worth and of rights as constituted of what respect for that worth requires are jewels bequeathed all humanity by the Hebrew and Christian scriptures.

On June 12, 1983, I received news that our twenty-five-year-old son, Eric, had been killed the day before in a mountain climbing accident in Austria. Nothing has so changed my life as that news. My life was at once divided into before and after. After I had recovered a bit from the shock, I decided to look for some books that might help me in my grief; that's what scholars do, they read books. I found almost all of them unbearable. They were about Grief, capital G, or about Death, capital D, or about The Grief Process. My problem was not with Grief; my problem was that I was in grief. My problem was not with Death; my problem was that Eric had died. I did not have questions about The Grief Process; I was grieving, and I found standing back to think and talk about the process obscene.

My own small book, *Lament for a Son*, which I wrote within the year after Eric's death, is not about Grief, not about Death, not about The Grief Process. It's not *about* anything. It's a *cry of* grief. I tried to be honest, not to say things that were expected of me even if I didn't believe or feel them. There's a lot of silence in the book, the silence of empty white space on the page. There are a lot of questions in it. A friend told me that there are almost as many sentences that end with question marks as with periods; I take his word for that. And a lot of it is image and metaphor, as when I said that sorrow was no longer the islands but the sea.

Eric's death changed my life. But did it change my mind? Did it change how I think? I had not thought much about grief previously. I had no occasion to do so—or better, I had not taken occasion to do so. But now, in various of my writings, I have looked at how we in the West, both Christians and non-Christians, deal with grief. What has struck me is how prominent is the strategy of *dis*owning grief, either by doing one's best to get over it or by denouncing it as sinful. I could not and cannot disown my grief; that for me would amount to disowning Eric. I loved him. If he was worth loving when alive, he is worth grieving over when dead.

And as for the theodicies produced by my fellow philosophers and by theologians, what now strikes me is that almost all of them are greater-good theodicies. For the sake of the greater good, God decided to allow some human beings to die young and some to suffer long and deep. I cannot accept this. What I find scripture saying is that God wants each and every one of God's human creatures to flourish until full of years. Did Eric's death serve some greater good? I refuse to think in those terms. My problem comes with that *each and every*. Eric did not live until full of years. Something has gone awry in God's world. I don't know why that is. I live the unanswered question. My writing out of these thoughts has been piecemeal and intermittent; I haven't known how to do better.

I have written a good deal about art over the course of my career, not because philosophy of art was a chapter in some system that I was developing but because art intruded itself, begging for attention. And I have written a good deal about liturgy, because liturgy intruded itself, begging for attention. To explain how these intrusions went would be to sound variations on a theme that I have now already sounded twice. My thinking has been in good measure from outside in rather than from inside out, and all the while the basic framework has remained intact. So rather than spinning off additional variations of the theme, let me bring these reflections to a conclusion.

The Kuyperian vision that I sketched out earlier presupposes that at the core of the Christian life is a dialectical yes and no: a yes to God's creation, and to all that is good in human creation; a no to all that is non-loving and unjust in what we human beings say and make and do. Christian existence requires Christian discrimination, along with the ability and willingness to say "This is good" to what is good and the courage to say "This must not be" to what is bad—the courage to say "This must not be" even when one is unable to say how it can be undone.

My reflections over the years on justice, grief, and other topics have led me to the sad conclusion that the ability of present-day American Christians to make Christian discriminations and to act courageously on those discriminations has been grievously impaired. Rampant in the American church today is the gospel of prosperity; preachers tell their congregations that what Jesus wants for them is earthly happiness and financial success; if they believe in Jesus, those will come their way. So what am I to do with my grief over Eric's death? Am I to conclude that if I believed more firmly in Jesus, I wouldn't be bothered by his death? Or what am I to do with my father's suspicion of wealth, conclude that either he didn't believe in Jesus enough or was insufficiently fond of money? I can scarcely find words to express my revulsion for a Christianity of this sort. We worship one who had nowhere to lay his head and who was obedient unto death, death by judicial execution. And now you tell me that this same Jesus wants us all to seek worldly happiness and financial success? I don't understand it.

And as to public life, what I hear many of my fellow Christians say and do is equally painful. When they get into politics, they all too often demean their opponents and tell lies with the worst of them; their only goal seems to be power for themselves and their cohorts. When they talk about national affairs, they talk about growing the economy, not about justice to the downtrodden. Yes, health insurance for all is expensive. But in a wealthy society like ours, surely every creature created in God's image and redemptively loved by God has a right to fair access to decent health care. When they talk about international affairs, they talk about national interest, not about what justice requires. Whether torture is useful has become a matter of controversy. But the question for those of us who are Christians is not whether it is useful but whether is it compatible with a human being's God-given dignity to torture a person. Justice is upfront in scripture. In the thinking and doing of many of my fellow Christians today, it is nowhere to be found. Love and justice weep.

3

Slow-Motion Conversion

CAROL ZALESKI

ON JULY 11, 1991, the Feast of Saint Benedict, I was baptized and received
as a Catholic in the chapel of the twin Benedictine communities of Saint
Mary's Monastery and Saint Scholastica Priory in Petersham, Massachusetts. Any views I've acquired since then pale in significance, washed out
in the light of the gospel and creed I accepted on that day. Yet a gradual
change began then and continues to the present, as I assimilate the effects
of baptism and confirmation. No doubt there are corners of my mind that
still haven't heard the news.

Mine was a slow-motion, book-driven conversion. For many years I
ran on two tracks. Along one track, I inched toward the church. I longed to
press forward, forgetting what lies behind, as Saint Paul writes (Philippians
3:13–14, a key text for Augustine's *Confessions* and thereafter for countless
narratives of Christian conversion), but nonetheless I held back, searching
and temporizing, out of respect for my Jewish heritage. Since my upbring-
ing had been wholly secular, whatever I knew of Judaism and Christianity
came to me mainly through reading. The chief influences were Augustine,
Anselm, and the monastic theologians of the twelfth century, in whose
writings I caught sight of a country I longed to inhabit but—I know this
will seem strange—didn't know where to find.

I met Christ in my studies, but it took much longer to get to know
the church. I found in the works of Marie-Dominique Chenu, Étienne
Gilson, Jean Daniélou, Emile Mersch, and especially in Henri de Lubac's

four-volume *Exégèse médiévale*, a Baedeker to this distant native land. But I had no inkling of the role that some of these thinkers had played as figures in the *ressourcement* movement that informed the Second Vatican Council. I knew nothing of the supposedly arid neo-scholasticism that was being overthrown—and is now being rehabilitated. I had barely heard of Rahner and Lonergan. I read Karl Barth enthusiastically but naively, as if he were a second Kierkegaard, and Hans Urs von Balthasar as a transmitter of patristic wisdom. I held a key in my hand, and it almost rusted there.

On the other track, I was a student of world religions, trained in the latest theoretical approaches—a devoted reader of Mircea Eliade, Rudolf Otto, Gerardus van der Leeuw, and Carl Jung, a student of classical Indian Buddhism, interested in mythology, iconography, philosophical yoga, folklore, and visual culture, and at the same time a product of a graduate theology program that involved grappling with Enlightenment and modernist thinkers. Studying world religions while reading medieval Cistercians and nineteenth-century Romantics gave me a taste for symbol and sacrament, but, unchurched as I was, I could not fully grasp the gulf between religion as object of study and the church as supernatural reality.

Funny things happened whenever these two tracks crossed.

In my first book, *Otherworld Journeys* (1987), I made a comparative study of medieval and modern accounts of near-death experience, highlighting the cultural factors that shape visionary experience. As a historical and comparative exploration, the book still seems sound. But there are a few pages in which I venture into theology and go off the rails:

> Theology . . . is a discipline of critical reflection on religious experience and religious language. As such, no matter how objective or systematic it becomes, it cannot escape the fundamental limitations that apply to religious discourse in general.
>
>   . . . although theology involves analytic thought, its fundamental material is symbol. Its task is to assess the health of our symbols; for when one judges a symbol, one cannot say whether it is true or false, but only whether it is vital or weak. When a contemporary theologian announces, for example, that God is dead or that God is not only Father but also Mother, he or she is not describing the facts per se but is evaluating the potency of our culture's images for God—their capacity to evoke a sense of relationship to the transcendent. . . .

> To say that theology is a diagnostic discipline is also to say
> that its method is pragmatic. . . . We must judge those images and
> ideas valid that serve a remedial function, healing the intellect
> and the will. In this sense, all theology is pastoral theology, for its
> proper task is not to describe the truth but to promote and assist
> the quest for truth.

You see, I was trying to acknowledge all the factors—medical, psychologi-
cal, and sociological—that contribute to mystical and visionary experience,
while removing the reductionist sting from such explanations. I was trying to defend the right of individuals to believe in their own experiences,
without resorting to protective strategies. I was trying to clear away the
obstacles to wholehearted religious belief and practice, while admitting
that religious belief and practice are culturally shaped. I thought William
James could help me with this project.

But what a jumble of half-baked epistemological ideas crowd the above
paragraphs! Despite what I said, I must not have believed it possible for
theology to be truly objective or systematic. Therefore I cobbled together a
Barthian sense of the unfitness of the human instrument, a Romantic value
for imagination, a mystical apophaticism, a commonsense pragmatism and
a false deference toward passing fashions (for, to be honest, I never took
seriously the suggestion that God should be described as Father/Mother,
let alone the idea that God is dead). The principle of divine transcendence
I invoke is unobjectionable in the right context—I might simply be echo-
ing Augustine's *si comprehendis non est deus* (if you understand him, he is
not God)—but the all-important countervailing principle of revelation is
occluded.

Perhaps this is understandable, for I was writing as an uninitiate,
whose relation to theology was idiosyncratic and bookish. Though by this
point I had read searchingly in the spiritual writers of the eleventh and
twelfth centuries, under the tutelage of Caroline Bynum and Arthur Mc-
Gill, my education as a graduate student in theology had been largely taken
up with Kant, Coleridge, Schleiermacher, Husserl, and James. I still love
these thinkers for their genius and good will, and feel immense gratitude
to Richard R. Niebuhr and the other generous teachers who introduced me
to them. Yet I lacked the means to systematize these diverse perspectives. I
was by turns a Christian Platonist, a neo-Romantic, and a historicist inter-
preter of the religious imagination. And all the time, the integrating vision
I needed lay hidden in the catechism.

Readers of *Otherworld Journeys* often say to me, well, yes, this is all very interesting, but what do you *really* think is going on in near-death experience? The short answer is that I consider near-death experience no different from other visions or private revelations, for which the standard methods of discernment should be employed, taking into account the relevant naturalistic explanations without dogmatically ruling out or credulously ruling in a supernatural origin. I am distinctly unimpressed by claims of the paranormal and consider psychical research a tawdry substitute for religion. My default setting when it comes to visionary testimony is at once sympathetic and skeptical. The right to believe is precious; the capacity for self-deception is boundless. My belief in life after death rests on entirely different grounds.

A better index of what I think as a Christian about death and afterlife can be found in the Ingersoll lecture I gave at Harvard in 2000 and in the little book, *The Life of the World to Come: Near-Death Experience and Christian Hope*, based on the Albert Cardinal Meyer lectures I gave at Mundelein Seminary in 1993. By then I had rejected the constructivism I was flirting with in 1991. To the "yes, but what do you really think?" question, I had a new answer to give:

> If God is willing to descend into our human condition, may he not also, by the same courtesy, descend into our cultural forms and become mediated to us in and through them? To deny that this courteous descent can take place is to reinvent the heresy of the iconoclasts.
>
> Such a *katabasis* would transfigure our all-too-human forms, so that they no longer serve merely self-serving ends; this is one test of a genuine religious symbol. But no matter how genuine, the symbol can never become completely transparent to the reality it represents. We cannot know what awaits us after death, but we can legitimately believe all that our tradition teaches and our experience suggests. We believe all this under correction, and—if we love a good surprise—we look forward to the correction.
>
> The truth about eschatology is itself eschatological. Now we see in an enigma darkly, in the mirror of our culture. Only "then," when the veil is lifted, shall we see face to face. Now we must test the soundness of our images and symbols by practicing the traditional and modern arts of discernment, guided by both dogma and experience. Only then shall we know as we are known.

I can almost trace my footsteps, in this passage, from the symbolo-fideism that kept me going through the 1980s and 1990s toward the theo-logical realism that has become my more settled lodging. The key word comes at the end: *dogma*. In the environment in which I was writing it was almost an incendiary word, but in my private thinking it was one of surpassing loveliness. Think *dharma*, I tell my Buddhist friends, and you will understand why the word *dogma* sounds beautiful to my ears.

William James, whom I have regarded as something exceeding an influence and approaching an uncle, ought to have made dogma anathema to me. If I were a true Jamesian, I should be writing about how my mind, unhindered by dogma, is incessantly changing. "The wisest of critics is an altering being," James writes in *The Varieties of Religious Experience*, "sub-ject to the better insight of the morrow, and right at any moment, only 'up to date' and 'on the whole.' When larger ranges of truth open, it is surely best to be able to open ourselves to their reception, unfettered by our previ-ous pretensions."

I still find much to admire in the intellectual humility of this passage. But the wisest of critics is an altering being, and I have altered mainly by swimming upstream against the currents to which James introduced me, from personal religious experience "immediately and privately felt" to wor-ship objectively offered; from theology as therapy to theology as queen of the sciences.

The dogmatism I now wish to recant is the dogmatism that blinds us to the beauty of dogma. Intellectual humility is one thing, but I began to realize that it is just as arrogant to withhold certitude indefinitely as it is to arrogate to oneself or one's cohort the power of attaining it. Certitude, in response to revealed truth, is founded on trust in the Holy Spirit, not in our own cleverness.

So I moved on, without alienation of affection, from William James to another nineteenth-century genius: John Henry Newman. Newman and James are kindred spirits in their personalist understanding of the search for truth, as well as their candid, affecting, colloquial, crystal clear, and be-guilingly convincing prose style. Yet Newman's famous saying, "To live is to change, and to be perfect is to have changed often," is worlds apart from the untethered experimentalism James espouses. Personal conversion, yes, this is the heart of the matter for both Newman and James; but considered in context, it's clear that Newman's saying pertains to how the mind of the church as a whole changes, by organic development of what is implicit in the deposit of faith—in other words, by the gradual unfolding of dogma. "From the age of fifteen," Newman writes, "dogma has been the fundamental principle of my religion: I know no other religion; I cannot enter into the idea of any other sort of religion; religion, as a mere sentiment, is to me a dream and a mockery." How I would love to introduce Newman and James to each other and hear them hash this out. In the meantime, I keep *The Development of Doctrine* and *The Idea of a University* on a small shelf of favorite books right next to *The Varieties of Religious Experience*.

My love of other religions has only deepened over time. Above all, I feel more Jewish than ever, thanks in part to the influence of our philosemitic Benedictine friends, the philosemitic pope John Paul II, and the experience of monastic psalmody. I understand more clearly than ever the urgent need to reject supersessionism and establish on unshakable footing the Christian recognition of the permanence of the covenant between God and Israel. I believe that the fidelity of Jews to Judaism is an essential part of the universal plan of salvation. I cringe when I look in our church hymnal and find those folksy tunes that vocalize the Tetragrammaton. My husband, Philip, and I have been reading Rashi and dipping into the vast ocean of the Talmud. I've read the Hebrew Bible in its Tanakh order (Torah, Prophets, Writings), though not, I confess, in its original Hebrew. Nonetheless, I have no wish to adopt an artificial dual practice. When I read the Psalms devotionally, I follow the Christological interpretation that is integral to the Bible of the church.

I feel an instinctive kinship with people of all faiths who are trying to live out of the heart of their religious traditions. It seems natural to make common cause with them on a host of cultural and social issues, including respect for human life from womb to grave. We have a close friend who came to this country as a refugee from eastern Tibet, where he had lived in a Buddhist monastery of the Nyingma sect from the age of five. He settled eventually in our town, married, and raised a family and has sustained the practice of his ancient sacramental religion. We see eye to eye with him and his family on the deepest moral and aesthetic questions, not least of which is belief in the reality of sin and the need for redemption.

It is a striking fact that, though conceptions of sin vary widely, all the world's religions recognize that there is something fundamentally awry with us, not merely maladaptive. I like this little ditty of John Betjeman's: "Not my vegetarian dinner, not my lime juice minus gin, / Quite can drown a faint conviction that we may be born in sin."

How else to explain our repeated failure to be human, the crude uses to which we put our exquisitely sensitive brains and hearts? Very little makes sense on any other view. But the belief in sin that Christians share with all traditionally religious people is fundamentally hopeful, for it implies that the cosmos has a moral structure and can be counted on to provide a means of liberation and cure.

I look to other religions not with a view to borrowing spiritual techniques or conceiving schemas of their ultimate unity, but simply because there is so much to learn from and admire in the integrity of a fully realized religious culture and in the works of holiness and beauty it inspires. I agree with T. S. Eliot that the *Bhagavad Gita* is, after the *Divine Comedy*, the greatest philosophical poem in world literature. Yet I have no desire—indeed, I have no right—to concoct a doctrinal or practical synthesis out of these or any other masterpieces of the great traditions.

Once upon a time, under the influence of some students of G. I. Gurdjieff, I overvalued the cultivation of attention (or mindfulness) as a religious discipline. I even proposed that attention could be a key to Buddhist-Christian dialogue. I am no longer so interested in that kind of interreligious dialogue. Once upon a time, I believed that Christianity was impoverished, compared to Buddhism, when it came to methodical spiritual disciplines. That was either ignorance or misplaced emphasis.

Once upon a time I planned a book on religious experience. If I were to salvage that book now, its subject would be adoration. Adoration is our purpose; it draws us toward our creaturely completion. While religious experience can be triggered by all sorts of constructs, images, and narratives, adoration is appropriate only in the presence of the absolute divine object, worthy of the bended knee and prostrate form. Adoration is supremely reasonable and objective; rationality is itself a form of adoration.

The shift in emphasis from subjective religious experience to objective religious practice is reflected in the book on prayer that I coauthored with my husband. We wanted to call the book *The Language of Paradise*, but the publisher opted for *Prayer: A History*. It is not, in fact, a history but an extended essay on prayer in its varied forms: petition, intercession, contemplation, liturgical prayer, penitential prayer, ecstatic prayer, literary prayer, and so on. We took issue with Friedrich Heiler's classic book on the subject, *Prayer: A Study in the History and Psychology of Religion* (1932), in which he says that prayer is "a spontaneous emotional discharge, a free outpouring of the heart" which by a "process of petrification and mechanization," eventually hardens into rites and formulas. On the contrary, we argued, prayer is a gift, but the life of prayer is the cultivation of that gift, not simply its spontaneous discharge; and the life of prayer in turn generates culture.

One still hears complaints about the "institutional church"—the very expression betrays a *parti pris*. But how would we know Christ without the institutional church? Who else would preserve the great secret of the gospel for us through the centuries, keeping it safe in the wilderness of opinions? We live in a world of institutions or in no world at all, and the institutional church is surely the greatest institution the world has ever known. It is the mediating institution between the family we are thrust into and the government that is either forced upon us or chosen by us from a distance. It equips us with every grace, every insight, every support for a decent life and then, like so many parents, is disappointed but not surprised when we turn around and say—we don't need you, we can do this on our own, you are a fossil, an impediment.

Do we have more reason to trust experimental, free-floating forms of religious life? Give me an institution any day, a big sprawling, international one, where authority resides in structures and traditions and is not invested in particular personalities; where my own personality is of little account, and yet I get to keep it. The ship of faith has its anchorage in the world, and I thank Constantine for it.

I believe that God's loving will guides the path of galaxies, subatomic particles, and human events. I believe in design, as Newman does, "because I believe in God; not in a God because I see design." And I believe that the design is marred by a Satanic power that works continuously to pervert it. But I am slow to read history suprarationally in light of this belief. Perhaps this is a vestige of the Tychism I took from William James, but I believe there is room for chance in God's design for nature and history.

The well-established findings of Darwinian science do not perturb me, especially when I reflect that ours is a fallen world in which God's plan for creation is obliged to unfold by means of death ("nature, red in tooth and claw"). How it might have been otherwise in an unfallen world, we cannot know.

I believe in the soul and continue to defend old-fashioned soul language against the dehellenization program that was fashionable in the twentieth century. I admit all that cognitive and neurological science can teach us about the physiological basis for consciousness and personal identity, but find that with every advance in this field, the mystery of self-awareness (the so-called "hard problem" of consciousness studies) only grows deeper.

I find much to admire in recent theological writing, especially when its expression is graceful, humble, free of academic jargon, historically sensitive, and not agenda driven. I'm drawn to contemporary thinkers who highlight self-surrender as the essential Christian disposition, but I don't think that this spiritual insight must entail the rejection of Cartesian, Aristotelian, or Platonic ontology. I'm glad to see that, after assimilating Karl Barth's purifying critique, many Christian thinkers are rediscovering the classic arguments for the existence of God and the permanent viability of natural theology. As ever, the mysteries of the triune God and of God's image in man are an inexhaustible subject for creative theological reflection. Nonetheless, I find some recent investigations of the inner, even erotic, life of the Trinity embarrassingly over the top. The best theological writing is slow to advance bold new themes. Always seeking to be true to the mind of the church, it arises out of and returns to prayer.

It's often said that we no longer live in an age of theological giants. Nonetheless, until the next age of giants comes around, theology still has its tasks to perform. There may even be some spiritual benefit from the loss of prestige. I like to imagine how theology would look if its production were, for the next decade or so, an anonymous affair. Then we would have no one to lionize as the successor to Athanasius, the courageous dissenter, or the discerner of new meaning-horizons for our time. Then theology could continue on its patient, plodding, pilgrim path, seeking God's face, alive to historical development, celebrating the rational beauty of the cosmos, reading the Bible in the light of the cumulative experience of the church, sensitive to social needs and crises but unfazed by passing cultural fashions.

As Augustine says, "I have been dispersed into times whose order I cannot fathom." Memory is unreliable. Yet if the two tracks I've been running on seem closer together now, and if (as I hope) there is more evangelical simplicity in my recent writings, I owe it mainly to the personal influence of my family, my godparents, our Benedictine monastic friends, and a few others. God only knows how far my mind has wandered off into the shadowy "region of unlikeness" or how far it has stayed the course, forgetting what lies behind and straining forward to what lies ahead.

4

Christian Claims

KATHRYN TANNER

WHEN I WAS IN the doctoral program of Yale's Religious Studies Department in the early 1980s (working primarily with Hans Frei, George Lindbeck, and Louis Dupré), the main worries of theologians and philosophers of religion were methodological in nature: Could religious thought and language be intellectually justified? Did religious thought and language, for example, meet general standards of meaning, intelligibility, and truth? One might argue—as Frei and Lindbeck did with an ironic display of academic rigor informed by the latest philosophy, literary theory, and social science—that they need not do so to be intellectually respectable. Epistemological issues (for example, how meaning and truth were conveyed linguistically through signs and symbols) and biblical hermeneutics were the bread and butter of our studies.

Methodological preoccupations distinguished theological schools (Yale and the University of Chicago) and informed the teaching of the history of Christian thought, another mainstay of the doctoral program at Yale. Frei and Lindbeck often half-jokingly quipped that one day they would eventually do theology, rather than spend all their time talking about how to go about it. But neither, it turns out, made much headway on that front while I was at Yale as a student and then as a faculty member during the 1980s and early 1990s. Any movement by Frei in that direction was tragically cut short by his premature death in 1988, and Lindbeck's energy was increasingly taken up with response to his influential and controversial

Nature of Doctrine, published in 1984, understood at the time not primarily as a work in comparative doctrine by a historically learned ecumenist but as the methodological manifesto of the so-called Yale School of Theology.

The hopes of my teachers for their own work came to fruition with the next generation of theologians, of which I count myself a member. Typical of this new generation of theologians—whatever their methodological commitments—is a willingness to make constructive claims of a substantive sort through the critical reworking of Christian ideas and symbols to address the challenges of today's world, a willingness to venture a new Christian account of the world and our place in it with special attention to the most pressing problems and issues of contemporary life. Pick up almost any work in theology at present and you are liable to find a discussion of the Trinity and its implications for politics, or a reformulation of God's relation to creation as an impetus to ecological responsibility, or a rethinking of the atonement in light of trauma theory. Frei, my old friend and mentor, at once so cautious and generous in outlook, would no doubt be astonished—grateful but perhaps a little envious, too, pleasantly surprised but also taken aback by the unself-conscious boldness of this new turn in theological inquiry.

Although my teachers might have been reluctant to admit as much, this shift from methodological to substantive preoccupations has surely been in part a response to, and general incorporation of, the lessons of liberation theologies. The Enlightenment challenge to the intellectual credibility of religious ideas can no longer be taken for granted as the starting point for theological work now that theologians who face far more pressing worries than academic respectability have gained their voices, both here and around the globe. Theologians are now primarily called to provide not a theoretical argument for Christianity's plausibility, but an account of how Christianity can be part of the solution—rather than part of the problem—on matters that make a life-and-death difference to people, especially the poor and the oppressed.

Postmodern trends in the academy over the past quarter-century have also encouraged this shift away from methodological preoccupations toward substantive theological judgments and their practical ramifications. The need to find theoretical justifications for the theological enterprise in particular has become less urgent given postmodern suspicions about all claims to universality, disinterestedness, and culturally unmediated insight. Appeals to specifically Christian sources and norms of insight and the advocacy stance assumed by many theologians are less suspect than they used to be, now that the tradition-bound, culturally influenced, and politically invested character of even the hard sciences has become an intellectual commonplace. Judgments in the natural and human sciences cannot be exempted from the scandal of particularity so often lodged against theology; any general outlook on the world and human life, whatever its basis and no matter how ambitious its scope, is shaped by contextually specific perspectives, topics of interest, and normative orientations. The burden of proof that theology once assumed alone is lessened because every discipline finds itself in the same seemingly inescapable circumstance to some degree or other.

With the chastening of pretensions to universal and disinterested knowledge comes a renewed stress on the practical character of rational judgment, since all claims to knowledge now gain a topical and situation-specific focus. Critical assessment of a claim requires consideration of who makes the claim, in what context, and for what purpose. In this academic climate, where a claim came from and the norms according to which it was generated are not as much at issue as critical assessment of the claim itself and what it has going for it. Even if sources and norms for theological proposals—such as faithfulness to scriptural witness—remain suspect in their particularity and relative immunity from criticism, thinkers believe that those proposals are saying something of wider moment about the world and our place in it, and as such are subject to challenge or support on a host of other grounds. Irrespective of their basis in sources and norms that Christians alone find credible, Christian recommendations for human life might well be plausible, aesthetically pleasing, practical, satisfying of basic human needs, and so on.

The question of the legitimacy of theology shifts, in sum, from theology's ability to meet some scholarly minimum in procedure to the question of whether theology has anything important to say about the world and our place in it. How might a contemporary Christian theology promote (or not) a more adequate understanding of the world and a more just way of living? What resources, for example, does the Christian symbol system have for addressing the financial calamity and environmental degradation we must now all face up to, whether we like it or not? How would the Christian symbol system need to be creatively and critically recast in the process?

Answers to such questions require new method, and in this respect method retains its importance. Theology's closest analogue can no longer be a perennial philosophy, addressing the most general questions of human moment purportedly common to every time and place, but rather sociopolitical theory. In other words, the theologian—like a Weberian social scientist or a Gramscian political theorist—now asks about the various ways Christian beliefs and symbols can function in the particulars of people's lives so as to direct and provide support for the shape of social life and the course of social action. The theologian needs a thorough knowledge of the way these intersections of cultural meanings and sociopolitical formations have panned out across differences of time and place—a thorough knowledge of the various permutations of the Christian symbol system in all its complicated alignments with social forces, for good or ill. Such knowledge in hand, the constructive theologian is better positioned to intervene in the current situation adroitly, effectively, and responsibly, with suggestions for both rethinking Christian claims and reconfiguring their import for human life.

My own theological trajectory has followed the general path just outlined in response to events of the times. I initially turned to theology from philosophy, which when I was an undergraduate at Yale involved (unusually for the time) the broad study of both continental and analytic philosophy and a familiarity with American pragmatism and process thought. The linguistic turn had been made, Thomas Kuhn had initiated a sociology of knowledge that chastened the objectivist ideal of science as a paradigm for all other disciplines, and deconstruction was in the air via the teaching of Geoffrey Hartman and Paul de Man and visiting lectures by Jacques Derrida; but the blurring of philosophy into anthropology and literary theory—now so common—had yet to take hold.

Theology held for me the prospect of addressing questions of meaning in a comprehensive fashion eschewed by most philosophers at the time. Theology as an academic discipline was clearly about something (not just talk about talk about talk), and its pursuit of the true and the right had significance for a community of inquiry outside itself—the church. Theology, in short, seemed to matter—to someone. Under the impact of postliberalism, which had begun to solidify around the work of Frei and Lindbeck, my work made that broader community of inquiry (which centrally involved religious people in their efforts to forge a way of life) its focus—as both subject matter and object for intervention—with a corresponding broadening of methods, away from philosophy as traditionally construed.

My first book, *God and Creation in Christian Theology* (1988), was a wide-ranging analysis of patterns of discourse about God and creation in Christian thought. It discussed the way such patterns of discourse modified habits of speech in the wider society in order to show (rather than explain) the coherence of various Christian claims about God and the world; it also discussed how those patterns of discourse were distorted and coherence lost under modern strain. Because Christian language was never adequate to the God to which it referred, the theologian was concerned not directly with that referent but with the habits of speech and action that amounted to God's direction of Christian lives. Intellectual difficulties arising out of everyday Christian practice—for example, the inability to resolve how I am to be responsible for the character of my life while dependent, nevertheless, on God's grace—set off theological questions about the compatibility of asserting both human and divine responsibility for our actions; and those questions were resolved by altering the way we usually speak of action in common.

In *The Politics of God* (1992), I more overtly discussed the function of religious discourse in Christian lives by exploring how beliefs about God and creation shaped Christians' political stances. Discourse analysis—the method of the first book—was insufficient here; the method was now something closer to that of sociology or anthropology. This book did not simply describe Christian practice (while commending it for its coherence, as the first book did). It argued a normative case—how beliefs about God and creation *should* shape Christian lives—in self-conscious opposition to the way those beliefs have commonly functioned to ill effect in the past and present.

In *Theories of Culture: A New Agenda for Theology* (1997), I raised up this new method as the primary subject for discussion, but only as a preparation for a more constructive, substantive agenda. *Jesus, Humanity and the Trinity* (2001) ventured a clear vision of the whole "Christian thing" (as David Kelsey, another of my Yale teachers, would put it); all the main topics of Christian theology, such as the Trinity, creation, covenant, Christology, and eschatology, were organized around the idea of God as gift giver, to establish a consistent Christian outlook on life and the corresponding character of human responsibilities.

Impelled by the horrendous events of 9/11 to address inequities on the global front, I developed the social principles garnered in that book from God's giving to us—principles of unconditional, mutual and universally inclusive benefit—into an economic ethic, again with an innovative methodical twist, in a subsequent book, *Economy of Grace* (2005).

This last book brought together all the elements of the historical shift in theological sensibilities I have been discussing. The inequities of global capitalism was the specific challenge that called for a systematic rethinking of Christian themes and their implications for economic matters. Fundamental Christian beliefs, for example, have often been understood to concern a Christ who pays our debts and a God who demands repayment for goods received, parceling out just deserts to those meeting the requirements of further divine favor by their proper use of previous benefits. Rather than seeming to bring a debt economy to completion in this way, might not Christianity instead portend its end by talking about a God who in Christ extends unstinting favor to undeserving sinners, offering them all, however foreign or alienated from God's household, the full inheritance of God's own children? Rather than accepting the terms of economic life set by the wider society, Christianity, I argue, would thereby be engaging in a cultural contest with it over what the fundamental assumptions of economic life should be.

Arguing on Christian grounds for conclusions that I believe anyone might find attractive, I suggest substituting common enjoyment and use of goods for the assumed need for private property, and the ideal of a community of mutual fulfillment for a competitive winner-take-all society. I develop a method of comparative or general economy, which extends the insights of French sociologist Pierre Bourdieu, to justify including in this way both theology and economics on equal terms.

Despite the idiosyncrasies of my personal trajectory, this sort of constructive focus on Christianity as a worldview capable of orienting social action and this investigation into the way such a focus requires conversation with social scientists are not especially unusual on the present scene. Liberation theologies, African-American, mujerista, and white feminist theologies, historicist- and pragmatist-influenced theologies, and those creatively developing a Tillichian form of correlation—these are often found moving in the same direction. One thing that sets my own efforts apart is the place of historical study for creatively reworking Christian ideas and symbols to meet present challenges.

Relevant to this interest in history is the fact that part of what originally drew me to theology was its oddity within the secular university and even on the contemporary scene (despite the recent rise of fundamentalism as a world-historical force). Theology had the ability to propose the unexpected, to shock and startle. It offered an escape from the taken-for-granted certainties of life by referring them to something that remained ever beyond them, resisting capture and encapsulation. The theologian respects that capacity of theology, it seems to me, not by dressing up contemporary commonplaces in religious terms, but in seeking what lies beyond a contemporary outlook and beyond the immediate context of one's work.

A theology that starts from, and uses as its toolbox for creative ends, materials gathered from the widest possible purview is, in my opinion, a theology with that imaginative expansiveness. Such a theology looks to the Christian past not for models for simple imitation but for a way to complicate one's sense of the possibilities for present Christian expression and action. It looks to the past not to restrict and cramp what might be said in the present but to break out of the narrowness of a contemporary sense of the realistic. It complements an understanding of the complex variety of premodern theologies in the West with an understanding of the complex forms of Christianity's global reach now and in the past. It moves beyond narrow denominational confines to the broadest possible ecumenical vision and sees beyond elite forms of theological expression, in written texts primarily, to the popular theologies of everyday life.

All that is what I mean by a historically funded constructive theology: the premodern, the popular, the global, and the ecumenical are put to use to shake up, reorient, and expand what one would have thought one could do with the Christian symbol system, in the effort to figure out what it is proper for Christians to think and do in today's world.

The breadth of this understanding of the historical, and the focus here on the historical complexity and variability of Christian forms of life, indicate ways that I have moved beyond my Yale training. At Yale the talk was commonly of *the* biblical world and *the* Christian tradition. I have also refused to understand Christian ways of living in isolation from the wider culture. Christian ways of speaking and acting are not created out of whole cloth but are constituted by odd modifications to ways of speaking and acting that are current in the wider society. It is therefore impossible to understand their meaning and social point without understanding the culture of the wider society and what Christian habits of speech and action are saying about it through modifications made to it.

For example, when Christians call Jesus "Lord," it is a comment on the lords of the wider society, a comment impossible to understand without knowing what is unusual about such an attribution in the context of its use. Contrary to its usual application, *lord* in Christian employment refers to a person shamefully crucified as a criminal and enemy of the state.

Similarly, the significance of eating in church is not clear until one understands the eating practices of the wider society. Modifications to those practices in church become a kind of critical commentary on social practices—for instance, a criticism of the exclusions of ordinary table fellowship.

Theological construction—figuring out what it is that Christians should say and do in the present context—therefore requires a highly complicated and subtle reading of the whole cultural field in which Christianity figures. One is helped here again by historical analysis (in my broad sense) that incorporates such a holistic cultural perspective. Theology is always a matter of judgments regarding the practices of the wider society and about the degree and manner in which they should also figure in Christian lives. Knowledge of how Christians have made such judgments at other times and places, and one's own sense in hindsight or at a distance about whether they did so correctly (for example, in suitably Christian fashion), provide invaluable insights and practice in tackling the issues of one's own time and circumstance when the personal stakes are much higher.

Method, I have learned, is no safeguard for making such judgment. Karl Barth was shocked by his teachers' support for World War I into rejecting the method of Protestant liberalism. I was shocked by many of my American theological colleagues' responses to the political upsurge of the Christian right in the U.S. and to the culture wars during the late 1980s and early 1990s, which so shamefully targeted gays and lesbians at the height of the AIDS crisis, into seeing that method (as it has been traditionally conceived) is insufficient. Too many of my teachers (meaning those already established on the theologian scene and from whom I expected wisdom and guidance) interpreted the upsurge of the Christian right simply as the salutary entrance of religion into the public square, promising an elevation in the seriousness with which theological exchanges would have to be taken by the wider society. *What* was being promulgated by the Christian right was of less interest.

Dismay and shame at the fact that Christianity could stand so publicly for this was not, as far as I could see, at a premium. Given at least superficial similarities between the postliberalism of my immediate circle of teachers and that of the religious right (for example, preoccupation with the world of the Bible, repudiation of apologetics, and opposition to liberal culture), the failure of postliberal theologians to criticize the religious right could easily be taken for an endorsement. To prevent silence from being taken for praise, the situation required, it seemed to me, only the most forceful repudiation of the Christian right's political judgments, something I tried to do in *The Politics of God*. The postliberal reluctance to be more than a witness to the wider society had to be overcome. It seemed to me, instead, that one's sense of that witness itself was to be formed in direct engagement with the political developments of the day. One should witness to a God who stood with those whom the Christian right maligned to further its own political interests—welfare mothers, sexual minorities, and the urban poor, for example.

I carried away from this time the belief that it is misguided to think that proper theological method will make clear all by itself the proper Christian stance on the contested sociocultural! issues of one's day. Search for proper method with that expectation encourages blanket judgments about the wider culture as a whole—it is to be resisted, or welcomed as the ground floor for the contributions of grace, or transformed as a whole—when what is really necessary is an often more difficult and nuanced discernment about particulars.

Advocating either the Word as norm for Christian judgment with Barth or critical correlation with Tillich does not help very much when the question is the contested one of how to read the situation in a Christian light in the first place. What, for example, does feminism or the movement for gay rights represent in Christian terms? An instance of moral irresponsibility, which Christians should resist, or a movement toward full human flourishing, to which Christians should be sympathetic? Such judgments have much more to do with the substantive character of one's understanding of what Christianity is all about than they do with the method used to come up with that understanding.

To make the simplistic parallel with Barth again, Christians supported the Nazis not because they neglected the Word in favor of cultural trends but because they had a misguided understanding of Christianity. Hitler's National Socialism was wrong on Christian grounds because its material policy toward Jews (and others) was unchristian and not because it forced the neglect of the Word by making an idol of the nation-state. Clearly, if its understanding of Christianity seems to warrant it, a nation-state can, according to its own lights, be trying to respect the Word while persecuting

Jews, and that fact would nevertheless merit as grave a theological condemnation as any the Barmen Declaration offers.

Christians are always influenced, one way or another, by the cultural trends of the day—respect for the Word does not exempt them from culture's effects (as Barth himself recognized in *Church Dogmatics* 1/2). It is what Christians do with these cultural influences that matters, as they grow into an understanding of their Christian commitments by way of complex processes of revision, appropriation, and resistance to them, taken one by one. One never rejects everything, since one's Christianity always remains parasitic to some extent on the wider society's forms of life. Nor (one hopes) does one accept everything, because Christian justifications even for courses of action shared with the wider society alter their sense and point.

One's judgments about different aspects of the wider society's practices need not, moreover, be uniform. For example, my grave worries about economic inequalities that are the product of global capitalism need not deny the greater economic opportunities for women that are also a feature of economic developments in the modern West. An equal resistance to both simply because they are the "world" that Christianity is to reject leads to dishonesty about the way that the world inevitably figures in even the best Christian lives and to a lazy reneging on Christian responsibilities to judge particulars with care.

Theologians need to be honest about the complexities of Christian lives and the way Christian beliefs and symbols figure there. Doing so means taking seriously what disciplines such as sociology and anthropology reveal: the often messy, ambiguous, and porous character of the effort to live Christianly. Trained historians of Christianity—particularly historians who avail themselves of the insights of those other disciplines—are not surprised by such a recommendation. Most theologians, I believe, have yet to see its force.

5

Lives Together

SCOTT CAIRNS

I AM SITTING IN a guest room of a monastery on Mount Athos in Greece, gathering my thoughts following two conversations with a wonderful monk. We spoke for a bit last evening and again this morning between services in the *katholikón*. I look forward to further opportunities to visit with him before I hike the rugged trail to another monastery tomorrow morning.

I mention my proximity to these particular blessings because they figure so prominently in shaping my response to the question of how my spiritual journey has unfolded. The availability of a spiritual father and the recovery of holy tradition has made me less inclined to see "my journey" as mine alone and more inclined to appreciate the vertiginous implications of our being the body of Christ, mutually incarnating our way into a collaboratively constructed future.

During the first of my conversations with the Athonite father, I mentioned my struggle with this very essay; I told him that a number of likely reconsiderations had occurred to me, but that I was keen to focus on one, and I also told him that I didn't want to squander an opportunity to teach myself a thing or two in the process of self-examination, in the writerly process of *coming to terms*.

This, after all, is one of the ways in which my mind has changed. Some thirty years ago, I still assumed that writers generally wrote to tell us what they knew; these days, I am convinced that the writers I treasure most are men and women who have written in order to see what they had not apprehended beforehand. Rather than understanding their art as a vehicle for transferring known matter from one mind to another, writers (and, ideally, the theologians among them) are men and women who trust their vocations as a *way* of knowing, or at least as a way of glimpsing the magnitude of what none of us can wholly apprehend.

Presumably, this is what every one of our vocations is capable of doing, as long as we remain true to their attendant gifts. Still, I can imagine how even a writerly vocation might go wrong, how a writer might—for instance—inhibit her own work or hobble his own engagement with language for fear of writing something that didn't fit with what she or he "believed." That sort of anxiety strikes me as pretty much the antithesis of faith.

I no longer view the sequential deaths and resurrections of life as matters of the mind, merely. Much as I am grateful for the late recovery of my smudged and recalcitrant *nous*, I no longer consider that profound intellective faculty in terms of the half measures accommodated by its commonplace translation—*mind*; and I therefore no longer imagine my metanoia simply as a turn toward better thoughts—as if our Christian faith were a simply propositional faith and not one that demanded embodiment, incarnation, fruit. You can imagine the sorts of endless splinterings and proliferative schisms that could occur over 2,000 years if one were to mistake Christianity for an idea or for a set of ideas. (In case you missed it, that was sarcasm.)

I was raised in a community that suffered a conflicted relationship with learning. On the one hand, perhaps out of feelings of intellectual inadequacy, our pastors appeared to study a great deal, affected scholarly demeanors, and sported honorary degrees. On the other hand, they did not appear entirely comfortable in that posture; they remained largely humorless, responded poorly to criticism and very poorly to questions, especially from the young.

We pored over the King James Bible, albeit selectively, and were treated to a sort of scattergun approach to word study, including both Hebrew and Greek words. For all of that, our pastors seemed to hold—and clearly encouraged—a deep suspicion of education, implying that too much learning could compromise one's faith. Secular universities were understood to be inherently evil, and the most prestigious sectarian universities were understood to be unduly secularized.

It wasn't until my days at a state university that I caught on to the poor scholarship that our community's puffed-up Bible studies involved, and it wasn't until recently that I have acquired enough Greek language and Jewish theology to mitigate some of the effects of our community's earnest error.

In retrospect, I would say that we put too little energy into learning who we were and too much energy into saying who we were not—a doomed choice.

In any case, I suppose that it is my sense of salvation itself that has undergone the most dramatic revision.

In his sermon on Solomon's porch—recorded in the third chapter of Acts—Saint Peter alludes quite matter-of-factly to what he calls the *chronon apocatastaseos*, or the restoration times. While his term *apocatastaseos* (nowadays more likely to appear in English as *apocatastasis*) was one borrowed from Aristotle, it proved to be a compelling provocation for most of three centuries of Christian discourse before, for the most part, disappearing from public view.

Such notables as Origen, Evagrios, Saint Gregory of Nyssa, Saint Maximos the Confessor, Saint Clement of Alexandria, and Saint Isaak of Syria, among many others, have engaged the notion as indicative of, as Saint Paul puts it, God's will that all men be saved. Even the Italian poet Dante Alighieri avers in his *Divine Comedy* that, finally, the flames of hell may prove to be nothing other than the glory of God, as experienced by those who have rejected him. Saint Isaak of Syria states in no uncertain terms:

> He acts towards us in ways He knows will be advantageous to us, whether by way of things that cause suffering, or by way of things that cause relief, whether they cause joy or grief, whether they are insignificant or glorious: all are directed towards the single eternal good, whether each receives judgment or something of glory from Him—not by way of retribution, far from it!—but with a view to the advantage that is going to come from all these things.

The saint says further:

> I am of the opinion that He is going to manifest some wonderful outcome, a matter of immense and ineffable compassion on the part of the glorious Creator, with respect to the ordering of this difficult matter of torment: out of it the wealth of His love and power and wisdom will become known all the more—and so will the insistent might of the waves of His goodness.

I'm with Saint Isaak. Still, as I recall, Christian Gottlieb Barth observed in the nineteenth century that "anyone who does not believe in the universal restoration is an ox, but anyone who teaches it is an ass." Duly warned, I won't press this particular beauty any further here.

So much for eternal damnation.

Over the years since first leaving home for college (more precisely, since my tardy discovery of the fathers and mothers of the church first led me to turn my eyes and my heart to the East), salvation itself has come to mean something larger to me, something fuller—both more substantial and more immediate than the understanding delivered to me by the community of my youth.

The way of salvation—as those fathers and mothers have taught me— is not the way of the mercenary (who serves to gain reward) nor the way of the slave (who serves to avoid punishment); rather, it is the way of the lover, who serves the beloved simply and purely out of genuine devotion.

For the monks on Mount Athos, "our being saved" does not have to do with an isolated instant of conversion, and its central benefit is not simply our being delivered from hell. The more traditional understanding of salvation is one that recognizes our moving toward and into a continuously thickening reality. C. S. Lewis's beautiful little book *The Great Divorce* offers an image of this—that of the human person shifting from airy shadow to illuminated substance.

Salvation is an ongoing process of redemption; it is our recovery from chronic separation from God, both now and ever, and it includes our increasing awareness of who our God is. The miracle has very little to do with the popular notion of "dying and going to heaven" and has far more to do with finally *living*. It has to do with our entering the kingdom of God, here and now.

Archimandrite Sophrony of the Holy Mountain, a monastic of the early twentieth century, offers keen and efficacious insight when he writes: "The essence of sin consists not in the infringement of ethical standards, but in a falling away from the eternal Divine life." Therefore the essence of salvation lies in our leaning into that eternal divine life, and our being in position to derive endless life from our partaking of the God Who Is.

The monks and their Orthodox traditions have insisted that this salvation is offered to all of humankind, not just to those few who acknowledge membership. Of course, the monks would be quick to insist that the most trustworthy, most satisfying road to full participation in the saving life of Christ is revealed in the traditional teaching of and participation in that One, Holy, Orthodox, Catholic, and Apostolic Church; they are also unshakable in the conviction that the One Body—that is to say, Christ's body—is synonymous with that selfsame church. We acquire our salvation through our being *of* that body, through our partaking of that body, and this strikes me as absolutely true, pretty much regardless of our meager apprehension of the matter.

Bishop Kallistos Ware famously parses this mystery: "We can say where the Church is; we cannot say where she is not." As Christ tells the earnest and anxious Nicodemus: like the wind, the Spirit blows where it will.

As I now see it, salvation has come to mean deliverance right now from the death-in-life routine that we often settle for, the sleepwalking life I have settled for in the past. Saint Isaac of Syria, writing in the seventh century, offers firm support to this promise in his *Ascetical Homilies*: "The man who has found love eats and drinks Christ every day and hour, and hereby is made immortal, . . . and while yet in this world, he even now breathes the air of the resurrection."

Inextricably related to this discovery is another developing sense that while salvation necessarily happens to persons, it is not to be understood as a merely personal matter. I continue to enjoy—and enjoy repeating—the surprising response given by my friend, a wise and kind monk, to a man who had come to evangelize the Holy Mountain and who asked the father if Jesus Christ was "his personal savior."

"No," the smiling monk said without hesitation, "I like to share him."

Thanks to the longstanding tradition this monk manifests, I see that salvation finally must have to do with all of us, collectively, and that it must have to do with all else as well—all of creation, in fact.

My reading in the fathers and the mothers of the church—assisted by my discovery of what I would call rabbinic, midrashic Bible reading—has me thinking that all of creation is implicated in this phenomenon we variously call salvation, redemption, reconciliation. Like the late theologian John Romanides, I aver that our saving relationship with God is quite specifically "as the Body of Christ"; our salvation is not a discrete, individualized, private bargain struck but comes by way of our continuing participation in divine life, as a member of a whole and holy body that is at once both alive and life-giving.

I have many friends who are, without question, serious, kind, deeply spiritual persons of one stripe or another; they also share a deep hunger for community, which they attempt to satisfy with a range of worthwhile activities. Oddly enough, they also share an abiding sense of alienation from the body of Christ, at least as that body is expressed in the media and quite often in their local churches.

Many of them have blithely said—albeit to my puzzlement—that while they may be spiritual, they are not religious. While I understand the unfortunate distinction being made by their strained parsing of terms, that distinction continues to strike me as the result of an ongoing failure—theirs, ours, and mine.

Somehow or other, these beloveds must find their way home. They must find a way to a reconnect their faith to their communities and their communities to their faith. They must find a way to reconnect, as it were, the spirit with the body. Satan, our tradition tells us, looks for any vessel sailing without a fleet, and—ironically enough—it seems to me that an individualized, isolated spirituality is almost by definition satanic.

I have been late in coming to this myself. In fact, my own difficulty with "fitting in" at the various churches I attended from my high school days through my early thirties left me floundering in the same isolated boat. I went a decade or so being a head without a body; I was a severed member, languishing alone.

These days, I see that we are called to work out this business together, and I see that faith is not something that can be both solitary and healthy. The health and eventual fruitfulness of the severed limb depends utterly upon its being grafted onto the living tree.

This is, in part, what I suspect Dietrich Bonhoeffer was hoping to reintroduce to his community in *Life Together*, wrestling as he does to reclaim the sacrament of confession. He writes: "The Christian needs another Christian who speaks God's Word to him. He needs him again and again when he becomes uncertain and discouraged, for by himself he cannot help himself without belying the truth. He needs his brother man as a bearer and proclaimer of the divine word of salvation. He needs his brother solely because of Jesus Christ. The Christ in his own heart is weaker than the Christ in the word of his brother; his own heart is uncertain; his brother's is sure."

His brother's word and heart—in the case of a confessor—are also informed by that most generous of democracies, the one in which, according to G. K. Chesterton, even the allegedly dead have a vote, that very cloud of witnesses whose writings, along with the holy scriptures, comprise the tradition that at once is our guide and provides our community.

Bonhoeffer insists that the presence of the brother—or, more to the point, the presence of the Christ borne in that brother's heart—shores up one's own faith, comforts and assures one's own trembling heart. It is the fact of their being "two or more . . . gathered in [Christ's] name" that enables their mutual apprehension of his assuring and unfailing presence.

This may be one of the reasons why, even among the monasteries of Mount Athos, the idiorrhythmic (individualized) rule has been set aside in favor of the more deeply traditional cenobitic (community) rule; the fathers' lives in Christ are necessarily *lives together*. Even the increasingly rare eremite, the desert dweller, in his bleak and rugged cave at the edge of Katounakía, regularly makes his way to the monastic enclave for the purpose of liturgical worship and communion. In the Orthodox tradition, there is no such thing as solitary communion.

This uncanny gift of a life together is not the property of monastics alone but is offered to us all. The more troubling point remains, therefore, that until each of us claims that gift and lives into it, the entire body suffers, and we—as severed members—are inclined to dry up as deadwood, no good to ourselves nor to anyone else.

"Ignorance and sin are characteristic of isolated individuals," writes the Russian priest Father Alexander Elchaninov. "Only in the unity of the Church do we find these defects overcome. Man finds his true self in the Church alone; not in the helplessness of spiritual isolation but in the strength of his communion with his brothers and his Saviour." Elsewhere this same priest offers a word of caution; quoting Saint Paul, he observes: "When one member suffers, all the members suffer with it. . . . If we do not feel this, we are not within the Church."

Dwelling somewhere at the heart of this lies the Christian understanding of the human person, an understanding that commences with the conviction that every one of us—of whatever religion or nonreligion—is made in the image of God, and that we all continue to bear his image, however well or poorly we do so. As the Orthodox like to say, we are all of us written as the icon of God.

The *One* God is said to exist in *Three* Persons engaged in a single *perichorésis*, a single circling dance, and our familiar—if inexplicable—trope of Trinity is our shared tradition's preferred manner of figuring God as an essentially relational being.

The image-bearing human person is therefore also necessarily a relational being. Safe to say, an individual is not the same thing as a person; authentic personhood stipulates the communion of one with another.

As for what we call salvation, it is better understood as neither an individual nor a future condition, but as a moment-by-moment, present mode of being—even as an ongoing acquisition, a developing realization. Maybe, in part, this is what Jesus was teaching when he said "the kingdom of God is within you." This may be what he was getting at when he announced, "I tell you truly, there are some standing here who shall not taste death till they see the kingdom of God."

Standing among his exponentially expanding band of followers were some "who would not taste death" before they had witnessed the kingdom of God, had tasted its power and were already savoring its abundant life, even as they hobbled with the rest of us through the valley of the shadow of death.

According to the fathers, this is a kingdom, a power, a glory, and a quality of life that is no less apprehensible now.

"The ladder of the Kingdom," writes Saint Isaak, "is within you, hidden in your soul. Plunge deeply within yourself, away from sin, and there you will find steps by which you will be able to ascend."

Archimandrite Sophrony asks:

> What does salvation mean? Do our bodies have to die so that we can enter the kingdom of Christ? How can we develop our capacity to live according to Christ's commandments, according to the Holy Spirit? Only one thing counts: to keep the tension of prayer and of repentance. Then, death will not be a rupture, but a crossing to the Kingdom for which we will have prepared ourselves by communion in the Body and Blood of Christ, by prayer, and by the invocation of His name: "Lord Jesus Christ, our God, have mercy upon me and upon Thy world."

In Abbas Isaak and Sophrony, I glimpse those who are speaking from within the kingdom already. The one who apprehends the reality of God's unfailing presence, the one who sustains ongoing conversation with his Holy Presence, is able to apprehend all things and all experiences—the good, the bad, the beautiful, the ugly, our loves and our afflictions, even our apparent deaths—as purposeful. That blessed pilgrim is able—even through his or her tears—to taste and to see that the Lord is good, that even our pain is remedial, that even our suffering is grace.

My own earlier struggles with a fiery temper have also been mitigated in recent years by an increasing apprehension of God's kingdom being here and now. Mulling all this over, I confess there was a time when pride had me thinking that every insult, offense, or error had to be corrected—by me, and immediately.

If someone were to treat me poorly, I made certain that person knew about it; if someone unjustly blamed me for any petty thing that went awry, the blame was duly delivered to its rightful owner.

Again, this is all in retrospect, but my subsequent practice of the Jesus prayer has helped me deal with these distractions in a very different way. For one thing, the prayer has helped me trust in God's unfailing presence, and for another, this trust—quietly but inexorably—has freed me from a perverse need to let my offender know of his offense.

Over time, the knowledge that God has witnessed these occasions with me allowed my anger to be replaced by something more like embarrassment, something like regret. Nowadays I feel complicit in the whole mess, sorry for our mutual, human error—and forgiveness goes without saying. The fact that an offender may remain oblivious of that forgiveness is absolutely beside the point.

And so, sure, I too want very much to be saved. These days that means that I want to be saved from what passes for myself. This is because what passes for myself does not always feel quite like the self that is framed in the image of God and is thus united with those around me and is, allegedly, growing with them into His Likeness.

I would like to replace this recurrently hamstrung, self-defeating, and sometimes isolated self with the more promising image: the person in communion with other persons. And while I'm at it, I wouldn't mind undergoing something like a lasting repairing of heart and mind, body and soul.

As I continue to discover more fully day by day, this journey toward wholeness is not something that one is able to undertake alone. Fellow travelers aren't simply a welcome luxury; they are crucial to our bearing our crosses as we seek to follow God.

Of course, we are likely to find that before we can set about healing the rift between persons, we have a good bit of interior work ahead of us in repairing and recovering the wholeness of our persons.

6

Reversals

ROBERT W. JENSON

So far as I can recall, most changes of my theological mind have not been changes from an established view to a contrary, but rather the result of encounter with a question or concern that had not before gripped me. I will devote the first part of this essay to a few items of this sort and somewhat arbitrarily set its *terminus a quo* at 1963, when I was thirty-three and had seminary, the doctorate, and a few years of teaching behind me. The second part will narrate a linked series of actual changes of mind, which I must reach back to an earlier date to tell.

Item: In the summer of 1963 I was hanging around Harvard's libraries, worrying about hermeneutics. Local civil rights groups were recruiting for a risky-sounding demonstration in Washington, and I thought maybe I should sign up, except that. . . .

On the last Sunday before the march, Henry Horn, pastor of University Lutheran Church, preached a sermon that moved me to immediate overt action—not a common event. The Gospel for the Sunday was the parable of the son who said "I go" and went not and the son who said "I go not" and went. When Horn entered the pulpit, all he said was that recruiting for the march was still open and how to get to the sign-up place. That afternoon several young scholars headed for Roxbury to sign up.

My experience of the great march was life-changing and the first of a series of events that politicized my wife, Blanche, and me. To be sure, our civil rights activism was itself comparatively undemanding. I taught at a college—Luther College in Decorah, Iowa—that immediately embraced the movement (our "protest" marches were led by the college president) and strained its resources to expand minority recruitment and establish ties with historically black colleges. And we were in England during the nation's most rigorous and frightening times.

Subsequent efforts against the intervention in Vietnam would be more strenuous. We returned to this country, for me to begin teaching at Gettysburg Seminary, late in the wild summer of 1968. We drove across the country listening to radio reports of the Democratic convention and the accompanying police riot. Gettysburg was handy to Washington: in the following years our demonstration clothes and kit were always ready to go. Indeed, Gettysburg became a sort of staging point for the marches. There were teach-ins and strikes at the local college and the seminary. I gave speeches in volatile environments, some with cops taking notes. We plotted. We made strange allies. Etc.

At more or less the same time a leftish Washington think tank recruited me as a consultant—they thought they should maybe know something about religion. And the venerable Leopold Bernhard, "pastor for political affairs" at Reformation Lutheran Church, just behind the capitol, made me a regular speaker in his sessions for inside-the-Beltway types.

When *Roe v. Wade* came down, we thought that protest against killing in an unjust war would naturally be followed by protest against killing children unable themselves to appeal for justice. But we, like others, were abandoned by our party and "the movement." This at once disordered and exacerbated our politics.

In the view with which all this has left me, Christian theology does not have "political implications" of the right or of the left, because the church's theology simply is its political theory—and indeed is the only true political theory. This does not mean that Christians will not disagree politically, but their disagreements will not be theologically neutral. And since there are some theological convictions that all Christians will share if they are faithful, there will be a few political positions of the same order.

What, for instance, is a "person," a word much used in some political theory? Standard doctrine teaches that what is true and good in God is the originating model of what is true and good in creatures; and in the church's doctrine of God—by no coincidence whatsoever—the notion of "person" plays a central role. Each person of the triune God simply is the third to the other two, established in its identity by its relation to them. Moreover, one of those persons is the mutual Word of the others. Thus a proper created person, as an analogue of triune personhood, can be neither the autonomous individual of much liberal illusion nor a mere item of a class or other mass; and the medium of the relations by which he or she exists will be address and response. A true polity would then be an arena in which persons were present to one another analogously to the mutual presence of the triune persons, engaged in discourse of the good.

Item: Three years spent teaching at Oxford, which in the 1960s and early 1970s was still the intellectual center of an intact (if barely) Church of England, had a major effect on Blanche and me. We were, of course, church folk. But at Oxford we came to experience the church as we somehow had missed doing before, as a reality just *there*, a sheer theological fact instituted by God. For one instance of our education, at a Eucharist in the chapel of Pusey House—where we had gone out of curiosity—the house master said in his homily that we should understand: whether these particular persons assembled again or not, he and the residents would be there, maintaining divine service. Consciousness of the church and its prayers as givens, prior to what individuals may do or think about them, has grown on us through the years since.

Item: I am part of the current revolt against the hegemony of "historical-critical" procedures in the exegesis of scripture. This does not mean I have turned against the practices themselves—they were in fact the vehicle of my initial access to scripture—but I have been made increasingly aware that historical-critical work cannot stand alone but must rather serve the church's intrinsic exegetical task: reading the Bible as a single book telling a single story—indeed, as a Christological metanarrative. This concern has even carried me into an unexpected new career: I have in recent years written two biblical commentaries, both on books of the Old Testament.

A final such item: Events have in recent years confronted me with the fact of Judaism in newly demanding fashion. The awakening has had two sides.

The one: I have realized how urgently the church needs a Christian theology of Judaism. It is all very well to renounce supersessionism, but how then *should* the church understand Judaism's continuing existence? In the next decades, powerful historical forces will drive Judaism and the church ever more closely together, and if they are to stand together, they will have to know why that is a good thing to do. It is not for Christian theologians to say how Judaism should regard its new partner, but the church on its side must find understanding that reaches far beyond good will.

I have been working at it. One key question Christian thinkers might ask themselves: since the church has become almost entirely gentile, can it by itself provide the risen Jewish Christ with a people of his own? Perhaps the risen Christ needs sisters and brothers who maintain Jewish identity in order to be himself, even when—or even because—they do not acknowledge him.

The other: in Richard John Neuhaus's colloquia and elsewhere I found that Jewish-Christian discourse need not be a mere exchange of views but can be a joint reflection on shared theological problems. I am working on that too, in various ways. This semester, a younger Jewish scholar and I are team-teaching a seminar at the local university on theological anthropology. And I cochair an institute, based in Israel and Princeton, that sponsors Jewish-Christian working parties on such shared themes as covenant and mission.

And so to the second, more narrative part of this essay, with its earlier *terminus a quo*. Assigned for my seminary internship to the Lutheran Student House at the University of Minnesota, I met and shortly fell in love with Blanche Rockne, counselor to the many flourishing programs then located there. Our first date—one had such things then—devolved into an argument about the World Council of Churches. As a self-consciously firm Lutheran, I was contemptuous of theologically pusillanimous Protestantism, which I presumed dominated the ecumenical movement. She had advised student groups at several state universities, necessarily in cooperation with other confessions. She won the argument and subsequently converted me to a principled ecumenism.

I could not at the time imagine what a train of consequences would follow one lost argument. In the event I have spent much of my career as a passionate ecumenist in the national Episcopal-Lutheran and the international Catholic-Lutheran dialogues: organizing conferences and study groups, speaking and writing on ecumenical matters, and co-hatching ecumenical schemes. I became and remain convinced that the original ecumenical vision, formulated at the WCC Assembly in New Delhi in 1961, represents the mandate of God: in any place where there are Christians, there is to be one eucharistic communion. It does not follow that all Christians in a locality must be alike in "ceremonies," only that they must enjoy some common oversight, be able to recognize one another's sacramental celebrations as authentic and be able to participate in them. Indeed, in my judgment, to the extent that this is not the case the very reality of the church is called into question.

In several of the connections just noted, mention must be made of the Center for Catholic and Evangelical Theology and its journal, *Pro Ecclesia*, which Carl Braaten and I founded to promote the central theological tradition regardless of participants' confessional affiliations. And as my last full-time appointment, I spent eight years as senior scholar of the Center of Theological Inquiry in Princeton, a hopefully benevolent spider at the center of what was in those years an international web of theologians of all traditions, an uninhibited ecumenical movement all its own.

A second reversal resulted from the first: ecumenical experience alienated me from extant denominational-territorial Lutheranism. I will name just one venue of the several in which this happened, the international Catholic-Lutheran dialogue. During ten years as permanent adviser to its third round of discussions, I was regularly appalled by Lutheran representatives' determination that nothing be proposed that would require actually changing anything in their churches' lives (the Lutheran cochair, Bishop James Crumley, was a splendid exception). I was further appalled by the Lutherans' lack of theological imagination or nuance as compared with the other party—I had thought it was supposed to be the other way around. For example, is it truly impossible for Lutherans to understand and in their fashion share Vatican II's description of the church as "a sort of sacrament" of general human unity? This may be the place to record that, looking into a book I published in 1970, I found that I had distinguished protestant and catholic "sensibilities" and identified the former as my own; now I would have to say the opposite.

I continue to regard Luther as one of the church's few truly necessary theologians and the sixteenth-century and early seventeenth-century Lutheran "scholastics" as a neglected treasure. The great potential contribution of both is their metaphysically revisionary Christology/sacramentology. How, for one central matter, are we to construe "body" or "space" if the eucharistic elements truly are the risen Christ's body? As theories, such construals as transubstantiation are only stopgaps.

As the West slouches toward nihilism, we can no longer depend on the surrounding culture's patterns of thought to provide a context within which the gospel's claims are intelligible. The church has to do its own revisionary thinking, bending metaphysics to the claims of the gospel rather than the usual other way around. The old Lutherans made a start.

But the way officially representative Lutheranism now uses its heritage—or rather a few slogans ripped from it—is another matter. For a central case: "We are justified by faith" is not the gospel. It is a doctrine *about* the gospel—the gospel itself is a *narrative* that makes a promise, the story of Jesus in Israel. Nor is justification by faith the one doctrine "by which the church stands or falls"; it is one of a number for which that might be claimed. And when preachers and the drafters of denominational statements try to derive the whole life of the church from this doctrine—or as it likely will be said, from "the gospel"—the necessary result is biblically untethered preaching, trivialized liturgy, and, perhaps most disastrous, culturally accommodated ethics and church practice.

If a *doctrine* is the gospel to be proclaimed, then the preacher has nothing to do but recite and explain that doctrine, never mind what the text may be about. Thus the famous Lutheran sermon template: fifteen minutes of moralism, ending with, "But never mind, God loves us all anyway, on account of our faith." If such biblical liturgical mandates as "Do this . . ." are law and not gospel, and if the gospel is all that finally binds us, then liturgical leaders are free to do whatever strikes their—often feeble—fancy. And if, for example, the biblical channeling of sexual desire is again law and only the gospel constrains us, then the church has no disciplinary defense against the late-modern sexual chaos that threatens its people also, including the ranks of its clergy.

Blanche and I remain members of a liturgically and homiletically exceptional Lutheran congregation, one that is unfortunately distant from Princeton, where there is no congregation of the Evangelical Lutheran Church in America. I remain on the ELCA clergy list. But we mostly worship with two Episcopal congregations for the sake of regular and recognizable Eucharist, the *Book of Common Prayer*, and generous provision of publicly read scripture.

One may well ask: why do you stay in this ecclesially irregular situation? As things stand, moving formally from the ELCA to the Episcopal Church would merely exchange frying pans. For a long time I regarded a move to Rome as inevitable. But to end this narrative I must report another reversal: we will not, we now think, become Roman Catholic, despite great empathy with formerly Lutheran or Anglican friends and allies who have.

I have written that all Western churches should be under the jurisdiction of the bishop of Rome, in his role as patriarch of the West. I have written that the universal church needs a universal pastor and that Rome is the only place for this ministry. I stand by all that. But I have never believed and do not now believe that one's soul is endangered merely by lacking full communion with Rome. Nor do I believe that a celebration of the Eucharist or of other of the mysteries lacks any reality or efficacy sheerly because the celebrant has not been ordained by a bishop recognized as such by Rome. Thus individuals—as distinct from churches—who are not in full communion with the bishop of Rome can and therefore must decide for themselves whether to seek it. That such individual choices are inescapable is among the punishments visited upon a divided church.

So why do we now decide to remain where we are, wherever that is? Perhaps we in fact do not have an easily formulated answer. Let me just say: stubborn, indeed now somewhat desperate, dedication to that original ecumenical vision and an accumulation of experiences and reflections, none decisive by itself, have wrought also this change of mind.

And then, who knows what yet may happen, perhaps as a result of increasing familiarity with Judaism or simply of some unexpected writing assignment?

7

Deep and Wide

MARK NOLL

IN SUNDAY SCHOOL MORE than fifty years ago we used to sing, "Deep and wide, deep and wide, there's a fountain flowing deep and wide." Perhaps our teachers knew what was flowing deep and wide, how to identify the fountain, and where whatever was flowing flowed, though I doubt if we kids who chimed in so enthusiastically had an inkling. Now, however, I find this simple chorus comes close to describing how my mind has changed over the last four decades.

The place in time from which I am measuring change is the period surrounding graduation from an evangelical Christian college, the first faltering steps toward an academic career, and marriage to Maggie Packer, who, forty years on, is more of an anchor than ever. Looking back now, it is clear that in this formative period an intellectual and spiritual home was being built for me of several different elements.

One was a growing sense that learning about the past was going to be my best means for understanding the present. Another was coming to realize that the evangelical milieus in which I found myself would be acceptable contexts for family, work, and worship. Still another was discovering through reading (Roland Bainton, A. G. Dickens, Gordon Rupp, Jaroslav Pelikan, Philip Watson, John T. McNeill) and through the conservative Presbyterian circles to which my wife introduced me that the classical Protestantism of the Reformation could provide a solid foundation for my faith and works. Most important was coming to experience the grace of God in

Jesus Christ as liberation from an existence otherwise enchained by the lust of the eyes, the lust of the flesh, and the pride of life.

In the decades since this construction process got under way, I have had no reason to deconstruct any of it, and many reasons to thank God for providing it.

Change, however, has taken place through coming to see how very deep and very wide was what, as a young adult, I was first given to glimpse. Yet as may be typical for those of us who are not expert at self-reflection, I'm not exactly sure how best to align changes of mind and the experiences that propelled change.

To the best that I can discern, "how my mind has changed" goes something like this: the basic dogmas of Nicene Christianity have become more important—they now seem truer—than in the hour I first believed. From that hour I knew that Christianity was deep and that it was beautiful. Now I believe that the depth is unfathomable and the beauty supernal beyond telling. I also have come to believe that no single word can describe the faith, though *dogma*, *story*, and *reality* all catch something of what is confessed in saying that Almighty God made "the heaven and earth"; that "the only Son of God . . . true God from true God" was the one "through him all things were made"; that this one "for us and for our salvation . . . came down from heaven" and was "incarnate from the Virgin Mary"; and that he was "for our sake" crucified, died, was buried, and rose from the dead on the third day; and that his "kingdom will have no end" as it is extended forever and ever through the "the Holy Spirit, the Lord, the giver of life."

The deeper and wider ramifications of Nicene Christianity are difficult for me to disentangle, because it has been through experiencing the unfathomable depths of Nicene Christianity that the surpassing breadth of classical Christian faith has become clearer as well. The changes represent an incremental growth in awareness over the years rather than illumination through specific events or striking eurekas. The experiences prompting these changes have been various, their effects cumulative, and their influences overlapping.

Academics too easily substitute bibliography for biography, but books have made a difference. So I'm able to see where I was helped by Martin Luther and John Stott on the cross of Christ, by C. S. Lewis on the subject of "mere Christianity," by Lewis's friend J. R. R. Tolkien demonstrating the power of narrative, by E. Harris Harbison and Herbert Butterfield on historical study understood in Christian terms, by James R. Moore and David

Livingstone on the supposed conflicts between science and Christianity, by Dorothy L. Sayers on the sanctity of daily work, by Boyd Hilton and Quentin Skinner on the embeddedness of all formal discourse (including theology), and in recent years by a great cloud of witnesses on the expansion of Christian faith around the globe. I am also aware of a more diffuse intellectual influence from the loosely organized American "school" that has promoted Abraham Kuyper's understanding of the lordship of Christ over all creation.

Yet even an academic knows that experiences beyond the page usually exert a greater force than what is written. For me, some of those experiences took place when I was a student. As an undergraduate at Wheaton College I learned from several professors how natural it could be to link serious intellectual pursuits with simple Christian faithfulness. At Trinity Evangelical Divinity School in the early 1970s I learned still more. Several faculty, led by David Wells, portrayed the faith as a thing of intellectual power and moral beauty stretching back over the centuries and—despite many blotches, missteps, and disasters—deserving full commitment of heart, soul, mind, and spirit. Then at Vanderbilt University I found out how much I could learn about things that meant most to me from professors and fellow students whose commitments diverged in small and sometimes major ways from my own. That realization accompanied a parallel awareness that though some of the historical figures I was studying were hardly evangelical in a modern American sense, they nonetheless exemplified the finest evangelical virtues and offered the most penetrating evangelical insights—in the etymological sense of the word.

When I returned to teach at Trinity College, a sister institution to Trinity Seminary, I enjoyed a year of weekly coffee sessions with David Wells and George Marsden, the latter visiting from his regular post at Calvin College. These casual meetings gave me much more than most postdocs harvest from a year of uninterrupted study. It was a direct experience of the same mixture of intellect and godliness that historical study was providing through other means—though both David and George seemed to have a better sense of humor than most of the great Christian figures of the past.

Through such educational experiences the beginnings of change were taking place: from thinking of the believer's general vocation in Christ and my specific calling to the academy as needing some effort to be brought together to realizing that my task was to discover already existing organic harmonies; and from conceiving the boundaries of "genuine" Christian faith narrowly to thinking that these boundaries might be capacious in ways I had hardly imagined.

These educational experiences were important, but not as telling as the common human experiences of marriage, family, church, and day-to-day living. To be the best that I can recall, gradual shifts of perspective came into clearer focus over the course of my fifth decade (1986–1996). For what were probably personal reasons but also because of certain conventions in postwar American evangelicalism, I once thought of Christian life as the arena where hard-won principles were applied, where a proper grasp of the faith was put to work in realizing the faith in practice. Without giving up that notion entirely, I came to feel that the relation between conviction and experience was much tighter, much more interdependent than I had once thought.

The change was from thinking about the truthfulness of classical Christianity, the beauty of its breathtaking drama, and the effort of Christian living as relatively discrete matters, to experiencing Christian truth, Christian beauty, and Christian life as a whole. Through this process, dogma was actually becoming more important, but the range of dogmatic questions that now seemed of first importance shrank considerably.

This shift took place amid circumstances in which God manifested himself more viscerally, through both absence and presence, than in disciplined study alone. As only a partial list, the situations included a wrenching church split; the death of my father, who in his latter years had become a very good friend; the death of a very good friend who had become like a father; and the confusing pain of other friends' dashed hopes. In these situations—where answers were scarce—the Christian faith remained no less real. In fact, it became more intensely real. But the sense of that reality came mostly through believing friends who stood alongside during dark days, through hymns sung and recalled, and through the celebration of the Lord's Supper.

Fellowship was the in-group word for what took on new force through those years. This standing together through duress seemed simple but was anything but. It was the "communion of the saints," not as the result or the product of what came before these words in the Apostles' Creed, but as an instantiation of those realities. First and always most important was communion in Christ with my spouse, then with a wide circle of friends, fellow church members, and associates at work. Our pastor in those years was a pastor indeed, a shepherd who certainly did some herding, but more important, stood with, prayed with, and wept with the sheep. I had had such a pastor once before, but not until these later years did I realize how much the empathic gentleness of that shepherd of my youth had done to maintain an opening for faith.

Hymns did not exactly take on new meaning; rather, I began to sense more clearly why the best had been so consistently moving since at least the early adult years of self-conscious faith. Regarded simply as texts, they could offer unusually evocative communications of strong theology. But the gripping force of the hymns lay in their affect and not simply in their words alone, in the more-than-rational conviction they communicated through the combination of careful writing and effective music. It could not have been a coincidence that in these years J. S. Bach became, as he has been for so many others, a kind of fifth evangelist. Sometime in this period I was also delighted to discover that Charles Hodge, the nineteenth-century lion of Princeton Seminary who has been so often criticized for writing theology as an exercise in scientific biblical rationalism, suggested on several occasions that hymns and devotional writings from the far reaches of the church could construct an entirely sufficient account of the Christian faith.

A significant bonus in thinking about why the best hymns worked so powerfully at cognitive, emotional, and spiritual levels lay in recognizing where these particularly gripping hymns came from. As basically a Calvinist myself, I nonetheless saw immediately that the best hymns came from many points on the Christian compass. Some were ancient (for example, Ambrose of Milan: "O splendor of God's glory bright, from light eternal bringing light"), some were contemporary (Margaret Clarkson: "He, who in creation's dawning brooded on the lifeless deep, still across our nature's darkness moves to wake our souls from sleep"). Some were heavy (Johann Herrmann: "Ah, holy Jesus, how hast thou offended . . . I it was denied thee: I crucified thee"), some were light (Fanny Crosby: "Jesus is merciful, Jesus will save"). They came from fellow Calvinists ("I greet thee who my sure Redeemer art"), but also from the winsome and zany Count von Zinzendorf ("Jesus, thy blood and righteousness"), from Mennonites, Disciples of Christ, Catholics, Pentecostals, independents, and especially from the implacably Arminian Charles Wesley ("Arise, my soul, arise, shake off thy guilty fears, the bleeding sacrifice in my behalf appears. . . . My name is written on his hands").

Such effective hymns went deep because they communicated the core dogmas of the Nicene Creed with unusual force. Concentration on those core dogmas made them singable by believers almost everywhere; the singing turned them into love.

A further broadening effect of the great hymns took me longer to comprehend. With the help especially of Andrew Walls's account of how the once-incarnate Christ has been, as it were, incarnated afresh wherever Christianity enters a new culture, I came to see something else. While the dogmas of these hymns were universal, the music that played such a powerful part in quickening the dogma was particular. Isaac Watts's "When I survey the wondrous cross" remained fairly inert words on the page without the tune "Rockingham," by Edward Miller, or "Hamburg," by Lowell Mason. I might find singing this hymn with a rock-and-roll melody or accompanied by a five-toned Thai xylophone an intellectual curiosity, but it would not be heartfelt worship.

Over time the obvious became clear: the hymns did their great work for me as they were sung with music originating from only about two hundred years of Western musical history (1650–1850). With music not from the West and with later or earlier Western music, the affect simply was not the same. Extension was the next step: if I was experiencing the universal gospel through a particular cultural expression, it followed that the same gospel could be as powerfully communicated through other cultural expressions, even if those expressions were alien or foreign to me. The experience of those who could be moved by a rock-and-roll rendition of "When I survey the wondrous cross" or by a five-toned Thai version of a similar hymn was, in principle, just as authentic as when I sang these words set to "Rockingham." Understood in this way, the hymns were making me at the same time both a cultural relativist and a stronger Christian dogmatist.

The experience that prompted the deepest reflection on the nature of Christianity and my own life as a Christian was regular celebration of the Lord's Supper. For years our Presbyterian church in the western suburbs of Chicago celebrated communion in the Scots' Form, in which congregants came to the front, sat at tables, and were served the elements by the elders. This experience in retro-Calvinism was powerful beyond words—in part because it was an intensely communal experience (we knew the joys and sorrows of many who moved forward to be served) and because it was always accompanied by music (we sang good hymns, some old and some new, that focused on the work of Christ "for us and for our salvation").

What drew this cyclone of emotion into sharpest focus was when the elder, almost always a man or woman whom we knew and loved, said in giving out the elements, "This is the body of Christ broken for you" and "This is the blood of Christ shed for you" or similar words.

Many years before it had been intellectually thrilling to read Martin Luther as he expatiated on the *pro me, pro nobis* ("for me, for us") of the gospel. Over the years, the intellectual frisson became an existential epiphany. I was (and am) not sure of the dogmatic details; none of the classic formulas that have tried to explain "the real presence" of Christ in the Lord's Supper seems entirely satisfying. But whether in Orthodox, Catholic, Lutheran, or Calvinist form, I became convinced that in the Eucharist God draws those who take part into the fellowship of his Son. If I was ready, if I was not, if my sins lay heavy on my soul, if I had a momentary difficulty remembering recent transgressions, if there were distractions, if attention was perfectly focused—the circumstances were far, far less important than the phrases ending with "for you," than the eating and the drinking.

Reflection on the force of what transpired so regularly drove me to the following conclusions. The Lord's Supper encompasses life so powerfully only because it speaks of events that really happened and dramatizes dogmas that mean exactly what they say. But being invited to share in the rite and enjoying the privileges of believing the dogma require a transforming experience of the whole person. It pushes vigorously against pretense, ego, pride, self-serving, irony, and all the other postures that come so easily to all humans—maybe especially to the intellectually attuned. It enacts emptiness being filled, guilt overcome by grace, strife restored to communion. It demands my soul, my life, my all.

Once again, however, as the depth of experiencing the Lord's Supper opened up, it did not take long to intimate also how wide the experience had to be. If it was true that God reached out to me through the celebration of communion, so it was true that he reached out to all who took part in the rite. I continue to believe that differences in how the celebration takes place—differences in theology, authority, practice, belief, and more—are far from insignificant. Yet it strikes me as still more significant that all who are called to the table are opened to experiencing the grace for which it stands and which it communicates. With considerable arrogance, I even believe that this account of God acting toward us in the sacrament holds true for fellow believers who regard it as only symbolic and even—through yet another mystery—for those few who do without communion entirely. Over the years it has been a useful exercise trying to voice these convictions in verse—for example, "Scots' Form in the Suburbs" and "Somewhere Every Day" (see pp. 61 and 63).

Brad Gregory's magnificent history of persecution in the Reformation era, *Salvation at Stake*, offers an especially compelling account of eucharistic realities. In that strife-torn period, it was most often differences over what the sacrament meant that made Europeans willing to die—and kill—for their faith. Western civilization has certainly progressed since the sixteenth century in abandoning capital punishment as a means to adjudicate conflicts over the Lord's Supper, but it has also suffered a great loss. That loss is retreat from our ancestors' knowledge that life and death are at issue in every offering of the wine and bread with the words ". . . for you."

To concentrate, as this essay has done, on Christian fellowship, the singing of hymns, and celebration of the Lord's Supper risks the common pietist error of understanding oneself only at the cost of forgetting about the world. But if space permitted, it might be possible to show how a stronger existential grasp of Nicene Christianity can lead naturally to heightened diligence in supposedly secular tasks (including academic work), stronger commitments to social service and political engagement, much calmer attitudes concerning science and religion, increased confidence in the scriptures, deeper engagement with family and those we encounter daily, and greater concern for world affairs, whether bearing directly on Christian communities or not.

Perhaps it comes more naturally for an evangelical, in the contemporary sense of the word, to offer the sort of personal testimony found in this essay than to say what such a testimony means for other people and other circumstances. The changes I have tried to describe, however, leave me convinced that since the fountain I sang about so many years ago is Christ, what flows from that fountain is immeasurably wide in all dimensions as well as incalculably deep for all humanity.

Scots' Form in the Suburbs

The sedentary Presbyterians
awoke, arose, and filed to tables spread
with white, to humble bits that showed how God
almighty had decided to embrace
humanity, and why these clean, well-fed,
well-dressed suburbanites might need his grace.

The pious cruel, the petty gossipers
and callous climbers on the make, the wives
with icy tongues and husbands with their hearts
of stone, the ones who battle drink and do
not always win, the power lawyers mute
before this awful bar of mercy, boys
uncertain of themselves and girls not sure
of where they fit, the poor and rich hemmed in
alike by cash, physicians waiting to
be healed, two women side by side—the one
with unrequited longing for a child,
the other terrified by signs within
of life, the saintly weary weary in
pursuit of good, the academics (soft
and cosseted) who posture over words,
the travelers coming home from chasing wealth
or power or wantonness, the mothers choked
by dual duties, parents nearly crushed
by children died or lost, and some
with cancer-ridden bodies, some with spikes
of pain in chest or back or knee or mind
or heart. They come, O Christ, they come to you.

They came, they sat, they listened to the words,
"for you my body broken." Then they ate
and turned away—the spent unspent, the dead
recalled, a hint of color on the psychic
cheek—from tables groaning under weight
of tiny cups and little crumbs of bread.

—Mark Noll (ca. 1985)

Somewhere Every Day

(after William Fullerton, "I cannot tell")

From South and East, from West and North they gather,
on foot, by car, in rickshaw, tram, and bus,
in health, in wheelchair, in joy, in sorrow,
relaxed, uptight, disheveled, and fastidious.
They come, O Christ, to you, to taste the body
that once for all was slain, to sing and pray
and take a cup whose balm brings life from dying—
throughout the world and somewhere, somewhere every day.

The words they hear when they have come together
are chanted, lisped, intoned, or simply said
and tell in myriad tongues with every accent
of body broken and of life's blood shed.
Mere words convey a gift of perfect freedom,
a debt of love that no one can repay,
a yoke of new and welcomed obligation—
throughout the world and somewhere, somewhere every day.

The spaces where they meet are huge, resplendent,
or huts and hovels all but falling down,
on Sundays jammed but often solitary,
both nowhere and on squares of world renown.
Yet all are hewn from just one Rock unbroken
in whose protection no one is betrayed,
which lets itself be smashed to bits for sinners—
throughout the world and somewhere, somewhere every day.

The hands that tender host and cup are youthful,
emaciated, worn, and manicured.
They take so little time, they bring so little,
to do a work by which so much is cured.

These hands that bring the Savior near are icons
of hands once torn in order to display
with lines of blood the names who come receiving—
throughout the world and somewhere, somewhere every day.

—Mark Noll (ca. 2005)

8

Washed in Grace

EMILIE M. TOWNES

I GREW UP IN a world in which the folks around me valued language. Family and neighborhood storytellers and teachers in grade school and Sunday school filled my days and nights with words, ideas, Bible stories, and conversations. Before I knew the term *poetic*, the poetic world helped me negotiate Durham, North Carolina, in the late 1950s and 1960s.

I grew up in a transclass neighborhood. My playmates' parents were teachers, principals, tobacco factory workers, secretaries, lawyers, home-based hairdressers, professors at North Carolina College (later to become North Carolina Central University), stay-at-home mothers, women of ill-repute, doctors, police officers, nurses, dentists, and those who "kept" the children of parents who both worked. We participated in school plays, diction competitions, and church Bible contests and were judged on our knowledge of the Bible verses *and* on our diction.

This wonderful and sometimes maddening world of words taught me much about ideas and how to shape and own them. I was taught to listen closely to and watch carefully the adults around me, so that I would learn to be responsible for what I thought and how I said it and to know how to do it well.

This was a deeply black religious world. It was filled with the smell of lemon polish on church pews and with nurses in white uniforms who helped revive those who got caught up in religious ecstasy and then collapsed. It was a world of fiery preaching and quiet preaching, good sermons, pitiful sermons, and exceedingly bad sermons. The choirs of my growing-up years ran the gamut from the marvelous to those that made a joyful noise to the Lord. In Sunday school, we were taught about the miracles of the Bible, the importance of faith, and that Jesus loved all the little children of the world—"red and yellow, black and white, we are precious in his sight, Jesus loves the little children of the world." I believed this (and still do) with all my heart and soul.

It was a religious world in which testimony was a way to cleanse one's spirit, and there was a decided difference between testifying to the joys and sins in one's life and bragging about what you have and what you'd done. It was one in which I was taught the importance of doing one's first works over. This meant periodically reexamining one's life—from beginning to the present—to tell the truth of who you have been so that you have a guide for where you should go. This request to think about how my mind has changed (or not) is such an opportunity.

In this rich world of words and religion, I tended to be a quiet child who watched and listened closely. I listened to the wonderful interplay of words that were at times sacred, at times irreverent, at times full of deep emotion, and at times humorous, with incisive wit and social commentary. I was a black middle-class girl in the South. I learned about racism from the black and white folks around me. It was an education that puzzled me, because racism made and continues to make absolutely no rational sense.

My parents taught me about racism without pointing to it directly. Every evening my mother would sit me down in front of the television so that she could watch the news while she braided my hair for the next day. I listened to Jesse Helms, who later became a U.S. senator but who was then an executive with the Capitol Broadcasting Company, spew racist diatribes against the integrationists and the "nigras" on WRAL-TV. As I became aware that he was referring to the loving and hardworking folks that I knew, I realized that there were (and are) people in the world that dislike and even hate me because I am darker than they are. That struck me as odd and sad at the time. As I've grown older, it has struck me as tragic and a tremendous waste of time and energy. Trying to understand hatred has been one of the most formative things I've done in my life, and I now know that it will remain a challenge until I draw my last breath.

I discovered at an early age that one must learn how to survive the small and sometimes large daily indignities of racism—and I learned how to negotiate them with creativity and sometimes humor while maintaining one's integrity and sense of self. This is where the church of my youth was so important, for it continually reinforced the message that I was receiving from my parents, my grandmother, and the adults in my neighborhood and school: you are a child of God, God loves you, God will protect you, and you are a child of worth who can do anything you set your mind to. In short, I was surrounded with loving and caring people; they were far from perfect, but they were relentless in passing along their care, and they taught that we must do likewise with others—that this was fundamental to being a Christian.

Asbury Temple Methodist Church (now United Methodist) was a small black mission church in one of the black public housing neighborhoods, or "the projects" as we called them. My earliest memories of Asbury Temple are from the time when Douglas Moore was the pastor. He preached sermons that made sense to a little girl who had a lot of questions. Sunday mornings were a time when the church was attended by many students from North Carolina Central, where my parents were teachers and eventually administrators. Reverend Moore taught us about a God of righteousness who does not tolerate or condone racism and segregation. He reminded us of the power of prayer and spoke about developing a strong moral soul. The church was alive with debates and strategizing and the Holy Spirit. It was in this space that I learned that the church could and should combine a lively and soul-deep spirituality with a vital and active social witness. This example has stayed with me over the years; when I refer to "the church" it is this model of church that echoes deeply in my soul. It is this church that I try to work with others to build.

As I grew up in this church, the war in Vietnam and school desegregation were twin backdrops to daily life. The Kent State massacre occurred in my last year of junior high school—Ohio National Guardsmen gunned down four students as they were protesting the U.S. invasion of Cambodia in April 1970. That fall I entered high school under a court-ordered desegregation plan. It was an enormously difficult year. Although Durham liked to think of itself as a progressive city, white flight took over. White parents refused to send their children to schools that did not have a white majority of students. The Ku Klux Klan, Black Panthers, and communists were all active in my high school, trying to recruit and radicalize students. That first year was filled with tension and fear but no violence.

When four white students were gunned down at Kent State, I became aware that not all lynching necessarily involves black folks. That was the first time I began to see the linkages between what we do at home and global realities. There were young black men in my neighborhood who went to Vietnam and Cambodia and came home in coffins. We did not demonize them or their service. We marked their deaths as service to our country. They were tragic heroes for paying the high price of defending our freedom and that of others.

But we teenagers did begin to question why. I not only saw but felt the deep connections between that distant war and what was happening in my neighborhood and high school involving issues of class and race. I learned that little happened in my neighborhood that did not have some connection to another part of the globe. I began to put together the ways in which hatred can create deadly structures that treat others as less than human and that sanction violence and war. I began to understand that I am part of a global family. It became important to understand how to put all of this together with my faith.

The changes in me and around me have often coaxed changes in what I think and how I respond. I use the word *coax* very intentionally, as my life and thought have usually been a matter of unfolding into change rather than a series of aha! moments. I tend to listen more than I talk. My friends and acquaintances are a rather eclectic mix, but I have always been drawn to people with strong opinions and lively minds who also have a great sense of humor and a deep spirit of caring. This has been a good thing throughout my life because I too have strong and definite opinions.

Perhaps the most profound experiences in my life that have caused me to look again at my beliefs are the deaths of my maternal grandmother, Nora Jane McPhatter McEachan McLean Jackson, and my parents, Ross Emile and Mary Doris McLean Townes. They were and remain great spirits in my life. Each of their deaths rocked me past my heart and into my soul. When my grandmother died in 1983, I learned that my deep and abiding sense of justice needed to be integrated with a vigorous understanding of grace. When my father died, I came to learn that my doctrine of sin was far too prominent and that I needed to have a more robust doctrine of creation. When my mother died, I learned that my understanding of salvation needed to be more expansive. With each of these losses, what I knew expanded and shifted. This grace-filled interplay of head and heart continues to shape me.

Each of these changes was marked by a gradual shift—I began to hear myself say new things in the classroom as both a student and a teacher. It is not surprising that the contours of justice were of utmost important to me as I struggled to make sense of the bold injustice of racial discrimination and other forms of hatred. From church to grade school I was taught that each of us has worth because we are God's children, and because we have worth we must respect each other and work to create a world in which this is experienced by all. My early sermons were infused with messages of social justice, exhorting people to be engaged in bringing in the kingdom in the here and now. I was clearly influenced by the ferment of the times and the strong message of justice-making I learned in my early years in the church. What I had placed on a back burner was spirituality.

The balance began to return when my grandmother died and a piece of my soul went with her. Her death was the first death of a close loved one in my adulthood. My grandmother was a rock in our family. My sense of being left behind to carry on was overwhelming. She had taught me well about the importance of living a faithful life and sharing the gifts I receive from God with others. Because she was certain, I was certain. Now I had to develop that certainty on my own and do so with the kind of integrity of faith she lived. Life for me was no longer so clearly marked out between good and bad.

As I mourned her passing, I began to look anew at the small group of black Christian LGBT folks I was working with as they tried to found a church. True, their lives revolved around issues of justice for all people regardless of race, sexual orientation, or class. But they were also struggling with questions about their worth: self-esteem, family acceptance, body image, and substance abuse. Justice was important, but I began to see that concern for justice must be tempered with grace. It was crucial that I helped them (and myself) to see the gift of unmerited favor from God and how this gift provides guidelines for living in which we must open up our hearts and lives to others with charity and understanding.

This experience has put me on a path of truly living what I first learned when I was a field-education student working with pastor and professor David Bartlett in the late 1970s: never speak a word of judgment without also speaking a word of grace. Both are required in ministry and in scholarship if one is serious about seeking wholeness for and with others.

Dad's death, just eight years later, was unexpected. My mother had noticed that he was declining but decided that she did not want to worry my sister and me. She called to tell me she had just found him in his favorite early morning newspaper-reading chair. I asked Mom not to have

Dad's body cremated until I could say good-bye. I rushed home in complete numbness and entered the funeral home with my mother and sister. I was struck with how small Dad was—he had shrunk some in death—and as I reached out to touch him, the first time I had done so with a dead body, I was surprised at how cool his body was. I kept hoping to see him draw breath again.

As we drove home, we began to share our feelings of those last moments with Dad's body and the ways in which he was wonderfully flawed. Later that night, as I struggled to feel past the numbness, the first chapter of Genesis began to blend with the first five verses of the first chapter of John. In the midst of my mourning, "and God said it was good" and "in the beginning was the Word" formed a prayer chant. It began to dawn on me that we spend far too much spiritual and theological energy on the doctrine of sin and not nearly enough time on the doctrine of creation. Yes, Dad was gone, but I began to realize that part of what I felt in the funeral home as I looked at his familiar face and hands was similar to what I feel when I meet a newborn for the first time—the miracle of creation with its endless possibilities for us.

Mom's death in 2003 was heart-wrenching. She had fallen ill over Christmas break and died in January. When I arrived from New York, I had no idea that Mom had suffered three massive strokes the night before and that paramedics had rushed her to the hospital. They revived her after each stroke—against her medical directive. By the time my two aunts and I arrived at the hospital she was having seizures, and it was difficult to get answers from the nurse on duty. It took most of the day before a doctor would explain what had happened. As my sister rushed home from Provincetown, Massachusetts, where she was in an artist-in-residence program, I cared for Mom by wiping the spittle from her mouth, and I talked with her as it became clear that she was dying.

My aunts—her younger sisters—kept a silent vigil as they watched another sibling slipping away from them. As the day wore on, I recalled an earlier hospitalization, when Mom had minor surgery and was struggling to recover from the anesthesia. I realized, as I fed her ice chips and urged her to progress to the popsicles, that eventually I would be in this position again. Now that time had come. As we spent that day together, I began to feel an overwhelming sense of God's salvation—more expansive and comforting than anything I had ever experienced. No, this was not the way that Mom had wanted to die. She had wanted no heroic measures and did not want to linger. But this was not to be, so God held all of us—Mom, my aunts, my sister, and me—as we held her into death. God did not abandon us, and this was beyond a deliverance from sin or evil. I became aware of the tremendous rebirth we were experiencing as we moved from life to death to new life. This was painful, but it was also comforting. Today I try to integrate this profound power of rebirth more intimately with the gift of deliverance as I teach and live.

I have learned that my story of faith must always be held in tension with the stories of others. As my mind has changed over the years, I am increasingly aware of how important it has been that these changes or unfoldings take place within communities—religious and not so religious. I have not been a solitary Christian for most of my journey of faith, though there have been times of what felt like unrelenting loneliness. The experiences of mourning I have described have an intensely personal as well as communal dimension. Ultimately, it has been the communal textures of this mourning that have helped me walk through my grief to find ways to lament and then to integrate the losses into living.

From my early years, faith communities have been the most important formative places for me as a Christian. As I have watched the extraordinary amount of ecclesiastical infighting that has erupted in recent years, I have become convinced that we need to stop trying to decide who is more holy or more representative of God's will or more closely aligned with tradition and instead place more emphasis on listening to each other as we express the hopes and questions that we bring to God daily. It is a form of arrogance to believe that we are right beyond question and that God speaks only to a select few. When we do so, we box God in, as though God is a divine possession rather than a holy presence. This denies the incredible gift of God's ongoing revelation in our lives and in creation.

Rather than practicing tolerance, we need to practice the wisdom that comes from recognizing our humanness. If the churches and its seminaries are to experience a renewal that is about more than counting the number of bodies in the pews, the size of the building, the spaces in the parking lot, or the color of the carpet in the sanctuary, they must abandon the need to be right and instead turn to God's call for us to be faithful. It is exploring this call to faithfulness that has shaped my ministry as I work with my students and colleagues to think through and feel through what it means to be part of the people of faith.

The call to faithfulness can help us shape theological education that prepares folk for a world that is more Asian than Western, more female than male, more darker-skinned than white, and less Christian, less equitable, and less well nourished than we are generally prepared to recognize. Churches and the expectations and needs of the people who are shaping them have changed and will continue to change. It is my hope that we have had enough of the pain caused by our need to impose narrow standards of acceptance and creativity.

I remain unconvinced that the mainline churches are in hopeless decline. I believe we are in the midst of a significant change in church and society, a change that many seminary and denominational officials and record keepers ignore because it is altering the model of church we are familiar with. Churches are mega, tall-steeple, medium sized or small, denominational or independent. They run the gamut from born-again to prosperity gospel to traditional to liberationist. Some are a combination of these identities. Too often our curricula support a pastoral model that no longer reflects what many churches are asking for or need. Yes, preaching and visitation are still important. But more and more churches realize that their ministries are calling for other skills, such as community organizing, political analysis, coalition building beyond religious organizations, and social strategizing.

Theologically, we need to think through what these skills require and how we prepare folk for leadership as we also continue to teach students about biblical reflection, about burying and marrying people, about denominational politics, and about how to get the furnace started when the pilot light goes out. We need to help students understand—and to remind ourselves—that theology is done not only by Karl Barth, James Cone, Gustavo Guitérrez, or Delores Williams. The children, men, and women in our pews who come with overwhelming questions at times also do theology. Perhaps the most faithful thing we can do is not rush to answer those questions or stifle them but rather listen to them, then take an amazing leap of faith and let those questions dwell in us for a season. In short, we can practice discernment and allow God's spirit, rather than human intellect, to guide us.

As I reflect on how my mind has changed, it occurs to me that it has always been the people in my churches and communities who have shaped me. Somewhere along the way, I came to realize that valuing institutions above people is bad for theology and dreadful for moral decision making.

It is important to figure out whether we are using what we call "faith" to abuse others and ourselves or are seeking to draw closer to God. We need an expansive sense of salvation and a robust understanding of creation, and we need to know that we are not dipped, we are not sprinkled, we are not immersed—we are washed in the grace of God.

9

Cross and Context

DOUGLAS JOHN HALL

FOR SEVEN SPLENDID YEARS (1953–1960) I studied at Union Theological Seminary in New York. Someone told me that visitors to the seminary were occasionally brought around to the tutors' office, where I worked as a graduate student, in order to glimpse "the Barthian"—of which species I was apparently the only one in captivity in that place. As such, I struggled with Paul Tillich, Reinhold Niebuhr, John C. Bennett, Daniel Day Williams, Wilhelm Pauck, Paul Scherer, and other luminaries of that unique period in Union's history—and therefore I learned a great deal from them. All three of the significant changes that have occurred in my thinking over the past half century could in some anticipatory way be attributed to their influence.

But it was indeed Karl Barth who, long before I went to Union, brought Christianity to life for me. I had grown up in the church, as one says, but Christianity only became interesting (well, indispensable) when, through the direct influence of one of Barth's students, I felt myself drawn into the "strange, new world in the Bible" as it was illuminated by the great Swiss theologian, along with others—especially Dietrich Bonhoeffer—whose faith had been forged in the white-hot crucible that was Europe in the early decades of the twentieth century.

Having acknowledged this foundational Barthian orientation, however, I must immediately demur: I mean in particular the early Barth—the

Barth of dialectical theology and the "theology of crisis," or Barth before his Calvinization (in the English-speaking world, his Presbyterianization).

It was more the critical, kerygmatic aspect of Barth than the later constructive, dogmatic aspect that intrigued me. Here finally was a Christian who could rekindle Pascal's "Fire!"—who could speak of a God "wholly other" than the gods of the philosophers and the prelates. He was as hard on "Christendom" as were Søren Kierkegaard and Franz Overbeck, both of whom he admired then. He said that doing theology was like trying to draw a picture of a bird in flight: you ended up with either an unmoving bird forever suspended in midair (orthodoxy) or an oblong blur (liberalism). Yet one knew even as he said this that Barth would not be able to resist the urge to try.

Perhaps, in the end, he was too successful. Much as I love vast passages of *Church Dogmatics* and believe that serious theology has to strive for comprehensiveness, I began early in my career to wonder whether Barth's courageous attempt to "see the thing whole" did not end in the former danger: a bird fixed in time and space—what Emil Brunner once called "a frozen waterfall" and Bonhoeffer termed Barth's "positivism of revelation." Certainly most of the self-confessed Barthians I have known have courted that danger.

Barth himself gave many demonstrations of his ability to rise above his own system. Yet a system it was, for all his protestations. And the first major change that took place in my thinking occurred when I realized that a great deal of what Barth wrote in *Dogmatics* and elsewhere just didn't fit the situation in which, from the mid-1960s onward, I found myself.

For a decade (1965–1975) I taught in a theological college (seminary) of my denomination, the United Church of Canada, located in what is (next to Quebec) probably the most politicized province of our country—Saskatchewan. It is the home of universal Medicare and other "socialist" dangers currently disturbing the souls of all Americans who are (in Michael Moore's apt phrase) in love with capitalism. My students were absolutely rooted in the grain-growing soil of that province—"stubble-jumpers," they called themselves. Besides, it was the sixties. If one didn't notice that one was no longer living in New York City or some other part of the mistrusted East, the characteristic events of that era, whether in Marxist or bohemian countercultural form, rose up and shouted at one—sometimes quite literally in the shape of aggressive students who seemed not to understand the polite ethos of seminaries in the 1950s: "Do you know where you are? Do you know what time it is?"

Like many in my generation of educators, I fought them for a time: They should please understand that they were called into a tradition thousands of years in the making! They should learn to listen before presuming to pontificate! But (partly because I began to care about some of them personally) I realized after four or five years that my students had a point: theology made in Europe, however beautifully and persuasively articulated, cannot be promulgated in Canada or the United States as though it were immediately applicable, with perhaps only a few local illustrations.

I began to see how imperceptibly I, though thoroughly a child of this "New World" myself, had been swept into the powerful narrative of European Protestant neo-orthodoxy, so called. My own nation's geography, history, sociology, politics, and culture had played a very small part in the evolution of my Christian understanding. What had occurred in patristic, medieval, Reformation, and modern Europe had had a greater voice in my theology than had the struggle of my own ancestors for a place in the sun. Like most North American writers and preachers, I had borrowed my theology ready-made from the sufferings of others. The uniqueness of Reinhold Niebuhr, the theologian I most admired at Union, only then began to dawn on me in all its epistemological fullness.

This awakening to my own context (I think I was among the first to employ this by-now-overworked term in theological discourse) also prompted in me second thoughts about Tillich, the greatest challenger of my seminary musings. Tillich too had created a system, and a captivating one. But it now appeared to me that his system, while intentionally and beautifully systematic, was in fact not as closed as Barth's; for in his "method of correlation" what Tillich named the human situation—which poses "the question" that "the revelatory answer" must endeavor to engage—by definition remains radically open to historical specificity and change. Without abandoning Barth (who, after all, also knew that the newspaper had to be kept in hand if the Bible were not to become an idol) I therefore turned with belated gratitude to the teacher with whom I had argued most.

What I was seeking, however, was something still more concrete. Tillich's sense of time was wonderfully sensitive: though a nineteenth-century man in many ways, he knew himself to be living (as he said) "on the boundary" of a quite different age. Because he opened himself personally to the moral as well as intellectual instabilities of that "shaking of the foundations," he could tell us about it with the brilliance and poignancy of a great novel-ist. (He did that best, I think, in his sermons and in *The Courage to Be*.) But in terms of his place-consciousness Tillich remained a European—specifi-cally a German, transplanted by circumstances at age forty-seven to New York City, which is certainly not America.

I began to find the language and nuance that I needed to articulate this discrepancy between our borrowed theology and our actual experience as North Americans when I noticed, after 1967, what was happening in the latest wave of Germanic theology. I refer to Jürgen Moltmann's theology of hope. My closest friend, the German pastor and theologian Friedrich Hufendiek, now of Berlin, introduced me to Moltmann's book before it had been translated into English. I loved it. But then, after its appearance in the English-speaking world, I was astonished at the manner in which, without grasping the foundation of the theology of hope in the Reformation's theol-ogy of grace and faith (without, in most cases, even reading Moltmann's difficult book), some liberal Christians in North America picked up the slogan "theology of hope" and ran with it.

Such an uplifting idea—hope! I found it appalling that a theology hammered out on the anvil of European despair (and personal suffering, in Moltmann's case) could so easily be co-opted by North American Chris-tianity's always eager market for happy messages. I wrote my first serious theological essay under the shock of that realization. I called it "The Theol-ogy of Hope in the Officially Optimistic Society."

Moltmann read my essay and invited me, during my first sabbatical leave in Münster, Westphalia, to visit him in Tübingen. I found him work-ing on his next book, which he saw as a corrective; for he too had discovered how Christians were misusing his theology of hope to bolster the cheap hope of religious answers that knew nothing of the questions—answers that in fact repressed the real questions. He said he would call his new book *Der gekreuzigte Gott*, and it would be an exposition of what Luther named the "theology of the cross"—a theology, as he said, "never much loved" but absolutely needed.

It was enormously encouraging to me that Moltmann, two years my senior, had been driven to explore again the *theologia crucis*, for I had embarked on this long sabbatical leave with the precise purpose of writ-ing a book about that much-neglected and even despised tradition, which Luther, who named it (but who was not its inventor!), had contrasted with theological triumphalism (the "theology of glory"). In the wake of my new awareness of the vital role of context in theological thought, as I cast about to see what kind of a response thinking Christians in Protestant North America might look for if they wished, as I did, to address the real but deeply repressed human despair of our context, I had concluded that it would have to be some indigenous articulation of just this thin tradition.

That it was that kind of Christianity to which I felt I needed to testify was both accidental and predictable. It was accidental in that I had no personal Lutheran connections whatsoever, but it was predictable in terms of my inherent spiritual and intellectual predisposition. I had always mistrusted the exaggerated and overconfident religious declarations of the dominant forms of Christianity and the moral smugness that invariably accompanied them. I had detested the bourgeois triumphalism that manifested itself in the "successful" churches of the 1950s. And on the positive side, I had always felt at home with strange figures scarcely known to the WASPish Christianity of my context—Luther (certainly, among us, the least familiar of the Reformers), Kierkegaard, Kafka, and Bonhoeffer (whose *The Cost of Discipleship* had been the first explicitly theological work I'd ever read). In fact, what I liked about Barth, I realized now, was the distinct hint of that same thin tradition still present in his early works, before the "triumph of the Third Day" took over.

Even if I had never heard any of those names, the *theologia crucis* had already claimed me when, as a young student of music at the Royal Conservatory in Toronto, I heard Bach's *St. Matthew Passion* for the first time. Anyone who contemplates the question why the Anglo-Saxon world is so everlastingly enthralled by Handel's *Messiah* and so unfamiliar with any of Bach's Easter or Christmas oratorios will understand why I felt that my vocation was to articulate a theology of the cross as gospel in the North American Anglo-Protestant context.

That, in any case, is how I saw my task as I sat down to write my first major book. While Moltmann was hammering out *The Crucified God* and Dorothee Sölle her *Suffering*, I was not far away in Münster trying to explain to myself (and hopefully a few others) why, as Paul wrote classically in 1 Corinthians 2, the cross of Jesus Christ is the center and basis of the Christian message; why it is not just a prelude to Easter; why, in fact, it must not be made null and void by the kind of resolution ("closure") effected by what I called our North American "resurrectionism." The resurrection, I felt (with Ernst Käsemann), is "a chapter in the theology of the cross." And what we are doing when we treat it as resolution is nothing more than an ecclesiastical projection of the ideology of success that drives the American dream and its paler Canadian counterpart.

The truth is that "man's story is *not* a success story"—words of Reinhold Niebuhr that appeared under his picture on the front of *Time's* twenty-fifth anniversary issue in 1948. The "religion of progress" (George P. Grant) serves only to blind human beings to the reality of their own and their neighbors' vulnerability, pathos, and suffering. When the Christian religion allows its witness to stray so predictably from the cross of the Christ to its "glorious denouement," it is simply lending itself to the deceptive project of the technological society—which is (as Ernest Becker so poignantly argued) "the denial of death."

When we turn the story of Jesus into a success story, we both cheat ourselves out of its depth and effectively banish from our purview all those (and they are billions now) whose actuality precludes their giving themselves eagerly to stories with happy endings. The gospel of the cross is not about rescuing us from our finitude; it's about a compassionate God's solidarity with us in our (yes, perhaps impossible) creaturehood and the slow grace of divine suffering-love which, without pretending finality, effects its social and personal transformations from within.

So with Moltmann, Sölle, and others of our postwar cohort I saw my task as one of recalling the churches to a theology that had unquestionable biblical and Reformation roots but had rarely surfaced as the core message of the Christian faith. However, unlike the Europeans and non-Westerners like C. S. Song and Kosuke Koyama, as a North American I could count on little or no religious or secular sympathy for such a message, for the churches here as well as the society at large were deeply and almost exclusively predisposed to the ideology of triumph. Even the American Lutherans, as Joseph Sittler once said to me, had forgotten the theology of the cross, though they have a sufficient memory of the *language* of that tradition that, unlike most Protestants, they at least do not find it utterly foreign.

Borrowing a phrase from Archbishop Cranmer's beautiful evening prayer, I called my book *Lighten Our Darkness: Towards an Indigenous Theology of the Cross.* I intended the title to suggest a little irony; for our darkness, I felt, was a hidden darkness that masquerades as pure light.

That book appeared in 1976, and the events of the past thirty-plus years have, I believe, made its thesis a little more accessible; for the success story of the North Americans has been profoundly battered throughout these decades, and there has been a greater openness among us to accounts of existence (including President Obama's) that look for light in the darkness and do not ignore or presume to banish it. I have not felt as isolated during these latter decades as I did when I first began to explore the theology of the cross for its pertinence to our sociopolitical reality. With very many of the theological-ethical trends of the past thirty or forty years (the various theologies of liberation, black theology, feminist theologies, gay and lesbian Christianity, environmental theologies, etc.) I have almost always felt common bonds.

At the same time, I have long wondered whether these many "theologies of," based as they usually are on specific issues, causes, or identities, necessary and exciting as they have been, have not had the cumulative effect of distracting the Christian movement in the postmodern era from its ongoing task of articulating a gospel that speaks to the human condition at its ontological roots, as Tillich did—and speaks to this condition as gospel.

The great question facing the residue of classical Protestantism in North America, I think, is whether it may be said to have a gospel. Too often the issue-and identity-based theologies by which much liberal Protestantism has been energized have been heard chiefly in the imperative mood—radical imperatives, and at their best luminous and right imperatives; but still imperatives—socioreligious analyses issuing in moral directives: law, but not necessarily gospel. In their passion for specifics, they tend to leave the whole untouched. Entire areas of life, and entire classes and conditions of human beings, are effectively excluded from their counsels (and communities)—except perhaps as guilty perpetrators of the wrongs that these theologies name (usually with right).

What I learned from my teachers—not only Barth, but Tillich and Niebuhr, too—is that the thinking that is driven by faith (*fides quaerens intellectum*) necessitates an ongoing endeavor to address creaturely existence in its complex and variegated wholeness. There is this comprehensive thrust in the faith because, as Havelock Ellis once put it, the "quintessential core" of religious faith "is the art of finding our emotional relationship to the world conceived *as a whole*." To this I would add a caveat: woe betide the theologian who thinks that he or she has actually and finally grasped the whole and translated it into propositions and dogmas and systems. As Augustine so wonderfully and succinctly warned us: *Si comprehendis, non est Deus!* "If you think you comprehend, then it's not God you're talking about!"

And yet the attempt to see things whole—at least to point intelligently enough to the bird in flight to help others see that it is actually a bird and not, for example, Superman—belongs to the life of faith as such and to the vocation of Christian theology in particular. Moreover, there is no reason why a contextually sensitive theology cannot at the same time make this attempt at comprehensiveness, the attendant dangers notwithstanding.

That is why I dared, in the decade preceding the millennial transition, to try to work out a contextually specific theology which at the same time addressed all of the cardinal questions by which Christian theology over the ages was guided in its search for a gospel that could speak to the human condition: revelation and reason, theology, Christology, creaturehood, ecclesiology, eschatology. For me, the exegetical core of this theology had to be the theology of the cross and, as the early Barth rightly observed, that theology is "a broken theology"—therefore a theology that defies, in any ultimate sense, comprehensiveness. So there could be no bravado in such an undertaking. But Christian theology must strive for the unity of truth even—or perhaps especially—when it knows that Truth is a living Word whose ineffability defies translation into ideas and words. Even a "negative theology" (and the theology of the cross is perhaps the only consistently apophatic theology that the West has attempted) must busy itself with critiquing what is false if the mystery that is the incarnate Truth is to be contemplated truly.

I shared with most of my generation of serious Christians the assumption that the Christian faith, sobered now by the various critiques of the secular world as well as those of its own best representatives, would increase—perhaps even numerically, but more importantly as a prophetic social force. Unlike our earlier twentieth-century progenitors we did not on the whole believe that this would be the Christian century, but neither did we entertain the thought that we might be living in the last days of the Constantinian era. Indeed, the postwar euphoria of the 1950s, with new churches going up on every corner of the suburban sprawl, encouraged many of us to believe that we were at the beginning of a new period of Christian relevance (a key word of the epoch).

Gradually, however, the evidence for such a vision waned. And by the end of the 1960s and into the early 1970s, in some parts of the once solidly Christian West the quantitative depletion of the so-called mainline churches made it virtually impossible to ignore the fact of a major shift in religious sensibilities. Not only were the old Protestant churches being sidelined, but

Catholicism too was losing ground. In Quebec, the year 1960 is usually indicated as the onset of La Revolution Tranquille (the quiet revolution)—a silent but dramatic rejection of the almost medieval Catholicism that had shaped French Canada. Canada generally began to look more like Western Europe in terms of both the numbers and the influence of Christians. Given the complex political role of Christianity in America, the decline of the churches was less conspicuous in the United States. But there, too, it was the older, once most established denominations that felt the icy winds of change.

The question confronting all of us who achieved some thoughtful awareness of this metamorphosis: What then is the mission of a church that can no longer count on its favored status in Western civilization to ensure its meaning and its continued existence?

I believed that the very first responsibility of Christian communities in such a situation was a) to begin at last to recognize the radical incompatibility of Christian establishment with the biblical and best traditional conceptions of the Christian movement, and b) to explore the possibilities of Christian witness and service from a position outside or on the edge of the dominant culture.

I remember a conversation early in the 1970s in which a small group of clergy in the city where I lived were discussing the question, "On the pattern of Revelation chapters 2 and 3, what do you think ought to be the 'message of the Spirit' to the churches of *this* city?" I found myself answering this question almost without knowing what I said: "The Spirit writes to the churches of North America: Disestablish yourselves!"

I'm afraid my words fell on the ears of my hearers as though I had been speaking in tongues. But I continued to pursue that theme in many lectures and in a whole series of books and papers on the future that I envisaged, with the help of many others, for a Christian movement that had seriously tried to disentangle itself from the ethos and assumptions of the imperial peoples of the West, with their explicit or implicit racism, ethnocentrisms, militarism, and ideologies of power. There is, I argued, a truly fundamental discrepancy between the concept of Christendom (the dominion of the Christian religion) and the way of the One whom Christians call *Dominus*. The secular world, in its way, had begun to intuit this incongruity before most Christians noticed it, and the sex scandals that had already begun to show through by that time only punctuated that "judgment that begins with the household of faith."

Instead of waiting for wave after wave of militant secularism, materialism, atheism, and so on, aided and abetted by the growing public awareness of religious plurality, to wash over them, the churches should take the initiative in their own disestablishment. Instead of clinging to absurd and outmoded visions of grandeur, which were never Christ's intention for his church, serious Christian communities ought now to relinquish triumphalistic dreams of majority status and influence in high places and ask themselves about the possibilities of witnessing to God's justice and love from the edges of empire—which is where prophetic religion has always lived. Instead of mourning their losses or naively hoping for their recovery, Christians who are serious about their faith ought to ask themselves why all the metaphors Jesus uses to depict his "little flock" are metaphors of smallness: salt, yeast, light—small things that can serve larger causes because they do not aim to become big themselves. I loved what a onetime fellow student at Union Seminary, Albert van den Heuvel, once wrote: "The real humiliation of the church is its refusal to be humiliated!"

Such a message, which is of course nothing more nor less than the application of the theology of the cross to ecclesiology, is largely still an unwelcome one in churches that not long ago were at the center of things. But it remains, I believe, the existential challenge of the present and future. The greatest dangers to human welfare in today's global village are all of them products of, or backed by, religions driven by immodest claims to ultimacy. A Christianity that still hankers after Christendom, as nearly all of us did until quite recently, can only increase the reign of death that is tearing our planet apart. Only a nontriumphalistic Christianity, an *ecclesia crucis*, can contribute to the healing of the nations.

Probably, if I am granted more years beyond my present eighty-two, my mind will change again. But I hope that it will always be change for the sake of distinguishing a living and therefore modest faith from the great temptation of all religion, which is to imagine itself true.

10

Faith Seeking Wisdom

DAVID F. FORD

MY WIFE, THREE UNIVERSITY-AGED children, and I spent last Christmas at a Christian center for genocide survivors in Kigali, Rwanda. We spoke at length with survivors of the 1994 mass slaughter in which about a million Tutsi were killed in a hundred days. We heard stories of whole families slaughtered by neighbors and fellow Christians, of women raped and mutilated and now HIV positive, of horrendous torture and humiliation. We worshiped with these survivors (an extraordinary mixture of tears, as testimonies to the genocide were given, and joy, as Christmas was celebrated with music and a survivors' dance group). We learned how the center helps with counseling, treatment for HIV/AIDS, education, housing, economic assistance, and, above all, with providing a kind of family for those with no family. We visited memorials and sites and talked to Rwandans and among ourselves.

As I have tried to absorb the experience, the genocide has seemed both more understandable than before and also much more mysterious and disturbing—and certainly not yet over, as its effects, its implications, and the attempts to come to terms with it continue. By comparison, the question of how I have changed my mind seems rather unimportant.

Yet the forming and transforming of minds, with their thoughts, ideas, ideals, intentions, attitudes, and descriptions of reality, is always significant—and certainly was in enabling the Rwandan genocide.

So how has my mind changed? One way of approaching the changing of a mind over the years is to draw, fairly arbitrarily, a dividing line between early formation and later transformations.

My formation included being brought up as an Anglican in the Church of Ireland in Dublin (a religious minority, only three percent of the population), playing a great deal of sports, and being gripped by the deep questions of life and death after my father died when I was twelve. It included studying classics (Greek and Latin) at Trinity College Dublin for four years; being active there in politics, debate, and student journalism; meeting a lifelong friend, the poet Micheal O'Siadhail (beginning more than forty years of changing each other's minds and hearts), and then nearly accepting a job to train as an executive in a large corporation. The business career was interrupted (permanently, as it turned out) when I took a scholarship to study theology at Cambridge. This was followed by a master's degree at Yale and then a doctorate at Cambridge on Barth's hermeneutics, with a semester at Tübingen University.

The result was a classical foundation (especially focused on text study, rhetoric, history, Greek and Latin poetry, Greek art and drama, and Plato) and a lively inner and outer debate about a range of theological issues stimulated by a variety of teachers—at Cambridge, Yale, and Tübingen.

What, apart from books, have been the mind-shaping surprises since then? What was to prove most transformative during the coming years, fifteen spent in Birmingham and then eighteen in Cambridge?

I went to my first teaching post at the University of Birmingham rather skeptical about whether I would like the city and almost at once fell in love with it. The years there were packed with new involvements: teaching for the first time and immersion in a remarkable Anglican parish (including five years as a church warden) located in an inner-city, multiethnic, and multifaith district. The parish work—with church schools, youth groups, home groups, a secondhand shop, and much else—was energized by a report called "Faith in the City," initiated by Archbishop of Canterbury Robert Runcie. My experience included work with a housing association that succeeded in renovating a large swathe of decrepit buildings, all sorts of university and city commitments, relationships with several Pentecostal and black-led churches through the Center for Black and White Christian Partnership, and marriage and children.

Inseparable from all this was a theological transformation that had a definite epicenter: conversations with Daniel Hardy. He was my closest colleague in the theology department, eighteen years my senior, widely read not only in theology and philosophy but in the natural and social sciences, literature, and much else, strongly committed to university, church, and city, and a profound, independent thinker. It was a theological springtime. We co-taught and did some other things jointly, but above all we set aside several hours every Thursday morning just to talk together.

Those conversations went everywhere: freely exploring, critiquing, speculating, arguing, proposing, imagining, deliberating, planning, and coming to verdicts and decisions. There was no question about what was central and comprehensive: the reality of God. To be able to think freely and hard about God and before God; to experiment intellectually and imaginatively together, alert to many disciplines, practices, and spheres of life, relating all to God; to take leaps and move fast but also to have the time to dwell on some particular thought, thinker, period, text, or problem for as long as we wanted—all this and more made up the "change of mind" I went through.

We eventually tried to shape and distill these conversations in a book, first called *Jubilate: Theology in Praise* (in its current edition, *Living in Praise: Worshipping and Knowing God*). It does convey something of the essence of those transformative years, which might be summed up as learning how to think freely and rigorously in constant amazement at and response to the superabundant God of joy, wisdom, and love.

The learning has continued, not least through celebrating Christmas with genocide survivors and through learning more about the dark mystery of evil, whose unavoidability, insolubility, and intractability had first been imprinted on my mind by my Cambridge teacher Donald MacKinnon.

Two further developments that took place in Birmingham have had long-term effects. The first was another sustained series of conversations, beginning later than those with Dan Hardy and still continuing today. These were with my Birmingham colleague in New Testament and patristics, Frances Young. We shared a background in classics and a passion for the New Testament, and our five-year collaboration on the book *Meaning and Truth in 2 Corinthians* proved formative for my own way of seeking to combine scholarship, hermeneutics, and theology in the interpretation of scripture. I am now trying to take this work further by beginning what is my greatest academic and spiritual challenge so far: writing a theological commentary (commissioned by Westminster John Knox Press) on the Gospel of John.

The personal was inseparable from the theological. Frances herself during these years was going through deep changes as she pursued her vocation to the Methodist ordained ministry and wrote the prose and poetry of her remarkable book *Face to Face: A Narrative Essay in the Theology of Suffering*, about her severely disabled son, Arthur. At the end of my time in Birmingham, Frances, because of Arthur, got to know Jean Vanier and the L'Arche communities he founded for people with developmental disabilities and those who live with them. She introduced me to them, and together we began a relationship with L'Arche that has grown stronger over the years. When I came to the final chapter of my recent work, *Christian Wisdom: Desiring God and Learning in Love*, I realized how deeply Jean Vanier and L'Arche have affected me. They had become a fundamental point of reference, the natural culmination for a book on wisdom in line with the gospel.

The second change was in my theological horizon. I undertook the preparation of a textbook, *The Modern Theologians*. A course developed by Dan Hardy that I co-taught with him was the starting point, but that did not cover the whole field.

The logic of the project, now in its third edition, led to my appreciating more and more the variety and productivity of theologians and trying to do some justice to their global scope, the number of relevant disciplines and media, the particularity of Catholic, Orthodox, Anglican, Protestant, evangelical, and Pentecostal traditions, and the significant new voices (women, African Americans, Africans, lower-caste Indians, lay Roman Catholics, Latin American farmers and workers, and many more). Looking back, I realize how vital a part of my theological education it has been to become literate to some extent in this range of Christian thought and practice, and in many cases it has led to meeting with the theologians themselves.

I have recently been asking myself, in the light of more than twenty years' involvement in this editorial task: What are the essential elements of theological creativity? The emerging answer involves wisdom in four interrelated dimensions: retrieval of the past (scripture, tradition, history); engagement with God, church, and world in the present; descriptive, critical, and constructive thinking; and creative expression and communication. One twentieth-century theologian who exemplifies all four dimensions in ways that are for me continually generative is Dietrich Bonhoeffer.

Moving to Cambridge in 1991 was a drastic change: a shift of teaching from undergraduate to graduate, new conversation partners, a whole new level of institutional responsibility, and far more national and international involvements in academy and church, and then later with other faiths. It was a very different intellectual ecology with some remarkably stimulating elements, such as the challenge of taking part in the most thorough transformation in the history of the faculty of divinity, engaging in cross-disciplinary conversations in colleges, serving on a promotions committee that covered all fields in the university, and every two weeks for twelve years participating in the Cambridge University Press multidisciplinary Syndicate, at which academics and editors scrutinized every book recommended for publication. This was an entree, via the readers' reports, into academic debates in every subject (and a constant reminder of just how little I knew).

Such responsibilities made it necessary to think hard about both the field of theology and religious studies and the shaping of universities in the contemporary world. Most of this effort was ad hoc and practical (policy debates with colleagues, syllabus revision, judgments on cases for promotions and book proposals, presentations to benefactors and other funders), but the questions pressed for joined-up answers, and slowly a future-oriented conception of the field and of the late modern university emerged.

Having been educated in theology in three very different university settings (Cambridge, Yale, and Tübingen), I became convinced that the uniting of theology with religious studies on the British model (as distinct from German confessional theology and the American tendency to separate theology from religious studies) is the most fruitful way to engage with the various religions in a university setting. It allows for a full range of relevant disciplines to be pursued, for questions to be raised by and about the religious traditions, and for conversations to take place between people of different traditions and none. In our complex secular and religious world such settings are vital for the sort of high-quality study, thought, and debate needed to encourage wiser faith and wiser secular understanding. It is a small but desperately needed niche in the intellectual and educational ecology of our world. And such thinking in relation to the religious traditions has a contribution to make to the shaping of universities.

As I looked at the medieval Christian origins of universities and their modern transformations, especially on the model of the University of Berlin, I was impressed by the need to rethink our conception of the university and above all by the need to incorporate wisdom-seeking (besides the seeking of knowledge and know-how) at all levels and in all fields.

My conception of the church changed during this period, too. It had in practice been largely local. But a series of involvements at other levels (being a member of a restructuring commission for a diocese, the Church of England's Doctrine Commission, the archbishop of Canterbury's Urban Theology Group, and the 1998 Lambeth Conference) and doing Bible studies for the archbishops of the Anglican Communion gave existential evidence of the value of those dimensions, even when fraught with conflict.

But the greatest surprise came in my involvement in interfaith activity. In the grassroots multifaith environment of Birmingham, I had become convinced of the great importance of the world's faiths engaging with each other conversationally and collaboratively (on the analogy of much Christian ecumenism). But I had not seen ways of doing so that allowed people to relate explicitly from the core of their faith, that enabled the engagement to be sustained long term, and that sought to benefit the rest of society beyond the religious communities.

Then, while I was on sabbatical at the Center of Theological Inquiry in Princeton, Dan Hardy (who by this time was both my father-in-law and the director of the Princeton Center) introduced me to the Jewish philosopher and theologian Peter Ochs. As a result, Dan and I sat in on meetings of a group called Textual Reasoning, cofounded by Peter, at the American Academy of Religion. We were riveted by what we saw: young Jewish philosophers and text scholars (of the Tanakh and the Talmud) engaged in argumentative discussion (with much humor thrown in) of classic texts and of works by such thinkers as Franz Rosenzweig and Emmanuel Levinas. Soon some members of the group joined with us and other Christians to form Scriptural Reasoning, and subsequently Muslims (led by Basit Koshul) joined too. The focus was on reading the Tanakh, Bible, and Qur'an together.

For several summers Dan, Peter, and I spent three or four days at a time together at Dan's family house at Twin Lakes, Connecticut. These memorable conversations, lasting morning till night, covered vast areas but always came back to how to conceive and practice scriptural reasoning. A core understanding of it was forged through the intensity of three-way engagement, with much argument and much laughter.

In between these meetings scriptural reasoning began to spread, with a core group having a milestone residential gathering on Long Island and then twice-yearly meetings, one in Cambridge and the other at the annual meeting of the American Academy of Religion. (For more on scriptural reasoning, see the website of the Society for Scriptural Reasoning and David F. Ford and C. C. Pecknold's *The Promise of Scriptural Reasoning*.)

Scriptural reasoning has transformed my understanding of both Judaism and Islam and led me to much rethinking of Christianity. To study the Tanakh and the Qur'an for hour after hour with Jews and Muslims who know and live their traditions; to be able to question, argue, and differ deeply but with respect; to try to see the Bible through their eyes and to articulate my Christian faith in response; to explore contemporary and practical implications of texts in all three scriptures (for prayer, ethics, daily living, teachings, philosophy, politics, economics); above all, to find deep friendships developing with fellow readers with whom I have considerable theological differences—all this has amounted to a fulfillment of what I was only partly aware of longing for while in Birmingham: long-term interfaith collegiality that can lead me deeper into my own faith, deeper into the faith of others, and deeper into commitment to the wider common good.

Strange to say, it is not mostly about becoming clearer regarding any of the faiths. I was much clearer about Judaism and Islam before getting to know so many Jews and Muslims. To plunge into a sea of Talmud or Hadith while trying to interpret a scriptural text is often more bewildering than clarifying, and to hear Jews or Muslims arguing among themselves subverts many textbook generalizations.

The same suspicion of neat religious packages has also grown in relation to my own Christian tradition. I increasingly see wise faith as a faith that is wary of the common dominance of clear assertions and imperatives but rather is exploring and, above all, desiring more and more of God's infinite and superabundant blessing, wisdom, and love. Desire for God and God's purposes is, I think, the embracing orientation of wise faith.

Institutionally, much of my first decade in Cambridge was spent on faculty and facility development, which included a new building, new posts and syllabus, stronger collaboration with the Cambridge Theological Federation, and the founding of the Center for Advanced Religious and Theological Studies. After the building was completed, it was possible to take a fresh initiative, and the Scriptural Reasoning group chose to concentrate on the three Abrahamic faiths. In 2002 the Cambridge Inter-Faith Program was founded—one of the most satisfying enterprises I have taken part in.

I have become increasingly convinced that the early twenty-first century is a *kairos* for interfaith engagement, especially among the Abrahamic faiths, and that there are likely to be serious consequences if we miss the opportunity. Asked recently to look to the future of theology for an article in *Modern Theology*, I named this as one of the five areas of greatest potential (the others were theological interpretation of scripture, the doctrine of the Holy Spirit, theology and the sciences, and theology through poetry). Like the ecumenical movement at its best, the massive interfaith challenge requires substantial institutional and organizational creativity, locally, nationally, and internationally, as well as conversation, collaboration, and thorough theological work and education. The thinking required for all this has hardly got going, and it needs above all to be done jointly through intensive conversation, study, and deliberation. As a catalyst for this I have not found anything as helpful as scriptural reasoning.

I spent nearly a decade on each of the books I wrote in Cambridge—a slowness that reflects both the ruminative way my thinking tends to develop and also the time I gave to other activities. The books were lifesavers, always drawing me back to fundamental questions, stimulating fresh reading and conversation, and encouraging the attempt to interweave the practical and the theological.

Self and Salvation: Being Transformed followed on from the God-centered *Living in Praise* by exploring how the self before God is to be conceived and to live, continually being transformed in the relationship. It is a theological anthropology that tries to perform in writing the sort of hospitable, conversational, other-oriented, worship-centered theology and ethics that I have found so fruitful. Its key trope is "facing": living in the Spirit before the face of God embodied in Jesus Christ (the whole book might be seen as a theological improvisation on 2 Corinthians 3:18 and 4:6) and facing other people in that light. Writing it not only allowed me to engage with both the Bible and some of the thinkers and saints who have affected me most—Emmanuel Levinas, Eberhard Jüngel, Paul Ricoeur, Thérèse of Lisieux, and Dietrich Bonhoeffer. It was also an attempt at a sort of theology that might fulfill the main aims of classical systematic or doctrinal theology, but do so through a set of genres that tries to unite the intellectual and imaginative, the philosophical and theological, the theological and ethical, the liturgical and biographical, and the traditional and contemporary. I think the main overall effect on me of writing the book was a sense of having found in a new way my own voice as a theological writer. There was more of a convergence of conversation with text.

That sense was stronger in my work on *Christian Wisdom: Desiring God and Learning in Love*. I decided to risk writing on the things that grip me most—the cries of scripture and of our world, suffering and joy, Jesus Christ and the Holy Spirit, God as the one who blesses and loves in wisdom, church, and worship—and some involvements that have occupied me over many years: scriptural reasoning, universities, learning disability. Above all, two inseparable, inexhaustible themes fascinated me more and more: love and the Holy Spirit.

The gift of the Holy Spirit, the sharing of God's own superabundant Spirit, the Spirit of Jesus Christ, is such a transformative reality that it is almost impossible to be sufficiently astonished at it or to take it sufficiently seriously and joyfully day by day. If this is our reality, doesn't everything have to be radically affected by it? How can we ever be sufficiently responsive?

I am brought back to the genocide survivors' center in Kigali. The six-hour worship service our family took part in on the Sunday after Christmas showed a blend of traditions, including the Pentecostal and charismatic, with praying in the Spirit and prayer for healing. The graphic testimonies about massacre, torture, and rape could easily have dominated the minds and imaginations of the seven hundred worshipers, and it was clear that recovery of anything like a normal life after genocide was a complex daily struggle. Yet the genocide was not allowed the last word. The ultimate word was sung, read, preached, prayed, and danced in the Spirit. This was the Spirit that had led Jesus the way of the cross before being poured out to overwhelm the disciples and others at Pentecost.

The experience of shaping one's life in the midst of being overwhelmed—by suffering, joy, gratitude, fear, truth, beauty, goodness, problems, evil, God—had been the main theme of my only popular book (and perhaps my favorite), *The Shape of Living*. Far more personal than my academic books, it is more concerned with ordinary living and was written during a difficult period in my life. Writing it, and sharing it chapter by chapter with a small group of mainly elderly members of my Cambridge church, St. Benet's, was not just therapeutic but theologically fruitful. The words were being weighed and tested against decades of Christian experience, and two of the draft chapters had to be completely rewritten. The group somehow gave me the confidence to speak from what was utterly central—the Bible, Micheal O'Siadhail's poetry, core relationships and experiences, what I had learned from and with my mother, wife, children, friends, and enemies, and prayer.

So what has my mind become through all this changing? That is not really for me to say, but the daily hope and prayer for continuing change is simple: Come, Holy Spirit!

11

Another Enlightenment

PETER OCHS

THIS ESSAY MIGHT BE titled "From Another Reformation to Another Enlightenment." Or perhaps, "How an Elder Thinker Returns to the Instincts of Youth." I have often detected the latter pattern in the works of other thinkers and have grown old enough to test this theory from within. Indeed, for the past two years or so I have begun remembering youthful dreams.

I recall entering college ready to embark upon the rationalist program of the Enlightenment: to become familiar with Descartes, Hegel, and, above all, Kant, as though they were long-awaited prophets. The appeal to my young mind was the Enlightenment combination of earnestness, desire for rational clarity and coherence, and hope that all the world could be conceived and lived as a universal symphony and, at least on some level, in potential agreement.

But my youthful hope was short-lived. I recall distinctly one night of intense disappointment when, after a summer-long study of Kant, it first dawned on me that this exhilarating universal vision was limned by the circularity of ego-centered self-reference. I don't mean personal ego (what Kant called the empirical ego) but the form of ego itself (what he called the transcendental ego)—a measure of all things that adopted the law of simple identity as its own measure, I = I. It was an immense disappointment, shaking what a young person thought was "all of being" to its depths. Are we forever locked in the circle of our own humanity? Is there no escape? Is there no true contact with the world, with others, with the real?

At the time I thought I was simply asking questions that all humans ask. It was only later that I saw my youthful inquiry as part of a historically specific tendency, characterized as "Enlightenment universalism" and displaying these beliefs: that rationality is identified with conceptual clarity; that the clarity of an individual universe "in here" (within the mind) corresponds to the rationality that inhabits and gives demonstrable order to the world "out there"; and that it is good for all of us to seek this clarity—this light—because it will be the means of our repairing what is broken in this world.

That is what Enlightenment meant to me in my youth, so you see why it is shattering to lose trust in it. Once one has left the garden of reason, where does one turn for guidance in healing all this brokenness? What is the appropriate direction and discipline for reason?

The beginning of life after youth came a few weeks later, in a flash, like a shower of light. It came after youthful months of reasoning, but it was not itself a reasoning. Rather, it was something like a passage in and through light. That's about it. My mind was changed not by itself but by some sort of shipwreck and some sort of participation in another economy of desire and hope and work.

I left one home—secular youth and love of cogitation—and entered a rabbinical seminary to acquire my grandparents' "home" of Torah. This meant coming home to Torah by way of *dikduk* (grammar), *shoreshim* (root words), *parshiyot* (weekly readings), *sefarim* (books), *peshat* and *derash* (plain and interpretative sense), Mishnah, Talmud, *halakhah* (religious "law," but a better translation is "pathways of action"), *tsibbur* (community), *tefillah* (prayer for which there are many words), and on and on. These pathways of work ended in *shabbat*, another garden, another childhood.

Paul Ricoeur calls it "second naïveté"—a helpful notion, except that I prefer a word other than naïveté. When it comes a second time around, it doesn't feel very naive. If I were a Pentecostal, I might use the phrase "second baptism" to describe it, but since there is work before the water, I'd settle for Mishnah Torah, "a second instruction that is also a second Word."

Some of us use the term *postliberal* to refer to this stage of thinking that comes after postmodern criticism—if one believes there is something that comes after. If there is, it cannot be a willful return to another modern dream of the universal and true; nor can it be an effort to romanticize a premodern tradition as if that tradition spoke directly to all human ears. These would be efforts to ignore postmodern criticism altogether by dressing up the ego in the clothing of some religious tradition and community or of some science of the universal. Postliberalism refers, instead, to an effort to discipline the *ego cogito* (the "I think") by reminding the ego that it did not give birth to itself and is not complete and true in itself. It was born out of others. If it desires clarity and truth, it will therefore need to investigate from where it received this desire, and the conditions for fulfilling it will lie in its source, not in itself.

Other postmodernisms also say this much. They may identify the source of this desire with a will to power or they may historicize it as part of some societal performance enacted at some time and place in response to some need or crisis.

Postliberalism takes another step, however. Its corrective genealogy traces the modern desire for light back to its Hellenistic roots—the consequence of a confluence of biblical and Hellenic desires. The biblical desire to serve the infinite will of God—the one creator of this world, the one revealer of ultimate wisdom, and the one redeemer of all humanity—is combined with the Hellenic desire to bring clarity to the language we speak and thereby disclose the cosmic truths to which it refers. When joined together, these two desires breed Enlightenment: the inspiring yet dangerous and misleading superdesire for humanity to reason its way to uncover the language of all languages and the speculative grammar of all grammars and to heal humanity of its failings and sufferings.

At that point in the genealogy, postliberalism turns from historical reconstruction to action: disclaiming this superdesire and in its place reaffirming the two separate and context-specific desires that preceded it. We may, postliberalism says, work to clarify our regional languages (and this includes modern languages as well as the scriptural languages Hebrew, Arabic, and Greek). And we must resume our service to God. But we must also renounce any effort to regard any regional language as if it were universal or confuse our human desires with God's. If we seek the universal, we recognize that it comes to us only through service to God, and God speaks to us only through finite languages and finite practices of knowledge and good works.

Nothing in this postliberal plan of action contradicts the postmodern critique of modernity. But by affirming traditions of action that preceded the *ego cogito*, this plan resituates reasoners within projects of service that postmodernists may, but need not, accept. Many do not.

And so I submitted the *ego cogito* to retraditioning. I found it hard work until I found I was not alone. After ten years of oscillating on the margins of academic philosophy and academic rabbinic studies, I found three companions (Robert Gibbs, Steven Kepnes, and Laurie Zoloth), then nine more and, after another year or two, forty to fifty more—all fellow travelers in postmodern or postliberal Jewish inquiry. These philosophers, Talmudists, literary scholars, and historians joined in the dual service to God's word and to finite disciplines of reasoning.

We began to meet twice a year or more to engage in what we called textual reasoning: a practice of poring together over rabbinic texts and rabbinic readings of scripture (*midrash*) until, around the table, over hours or days, the chains of discussions and arguments and discoveries about these texts and their interrelations and meanings seemed to take on directions of their own.

I am not referring to agreements among us (there weren't too many of those) but something like a style of intellectual (or cognitive and spiritual) dance, a rhythm we could not name but could recognize when we experienced it again. The rhythm included tropes and interpretive tendencies from each text we studied, aspects of each of our personalities as thinkers and readers, and some marks of the different scholarly tools we employed. But the rhythm belonged to none of these. It displayed the patterns of rabbinic reasoning from those texts and among those scholars on those days of study. Afterward, we each might write about these texts and reasonings in our different ways, but we became through the process (and for a time) a kind of community of inquiry and of mutual care. That community—or those sets of relations to texts and to each other—was the author of our textual reasoning; no ego or set of egos was the source of its unity.

Somewhere early in the life of what we called our Society for Textual Reasoning we discovered that Jews were not the only thinkers who engaged in a project of postliberal studies. Some Christians and Muslims did the same. They formed not only circles of traditional scriptural study but also circles of textual reasoners who knew the Enlightenment model of reasoning, knew the antimodern religious alternatives—and sought another way. While they might at times explore similar models of reasoning, they gathered around different canons of scripture and different traditions, or at times subtraditions, of interpretation.

We also observed that students of the different Abrahamic traditions often found it helpful to discuss with one another what they experienced in their study circles. Some spoke of comparable experiences of that rhythm of interpretive reasoning we saw in Jewish textual reasoning.

As David Ford mentions in his essay (chapter 10), he, the late Daniel Hardy, and I began to meet regularly to discuss these experiences. By dint of personality as well as tradition, we shared different but complementary approaches to the discussion. I recall, for example, that David drew our attention to the activity of the Spirit in these circles, to the poetics of our text studies, and to the broader theopolitical implications of such work in both the denominations and the academy. Daniel drew our attention to the energies of divine attraction, to the ecclesial and eucharistic implications of "drawing around God's word," and to the implications of scripture study for both theological and scientific reasoning. I argued that my Anglican friends offered a pneumatological approach to scriptural theology that complemented the christological approach of the American postliberals I had befriended earlier (George Lindbeck, Hans Frei, Stanley Hauerwas, and the students of these scholars). The three of us began to look over each other's shoulders as we studied scripture, and gradually we had began to practice the "study across borders" we later called scriptural reasoning.

We invited others from the United Kingdom and North America to join us in exploring this practice. By 1994, we had formed the Society of Scriptural Reasoning (SSR). During this period the Sunni scholar Basit Koshul became one of my Ph.D. students at Drew University and introduced me to a circle of what we later called Qur'anic textual reasoners. Soon several Methodist Ph.D. students (among them William Elkins and the late Roger Badham) joined Basit and me in a form of Abrahamic scriptural reasoning. In 1996, Basit brought a circle of Muslim scholars to help us make the SSR an inter-Abrahamic community of inquiry.

The members of the SSR realized how unusual it was for people to examine three different scriptural canons together and offer comments directly on one another's canons. This was not so unusual in a strictly academic setting in which each canon is examined at arm's length through text-historical and comparative studies. But the SSR invited all modes of inquiry, including commentaries emerging out of ancient traditions of religious practice. We did not worship together, but we brought our individually traditioned hearts to the table—hearts in dialogue with our academic minds, if you will.

In the process, we appeared to generate a third something: on one hand, a kind of believing practice, but a practice a step cooler than the practices of intradenominational textual reasoning; on the other hand, a kind of critical academic practice, but one open to the voices of our various traditions. We studied only within small circles that met for hours and days at a time and remained together for many years. We consciously nurtured friendships as an integral part of the study—friendships with one another and, metaphorically, among the various religious beliefs and practices.

Now my mind is changing once again. The first major change was that dramatic turn in my youth when, in a flash, my disillusionment with Enlightenment was met by the light of another way of knowing. This second change appears undramatic. It involves the gradual sense that, for me at least, the fruit of an adult lifetime of postliberal inquiry may be another enlightenment. I begin to sense that, when practiced in a disciplined way as an occasional complement to tradition-specific textual reasoning, Abrahamic scriptural reasoning may answer the desire I once had for the Enlightenment: the desire for that "clear and universal" reasoning that would be a light of truth and a salve to all of humanity's wounds.

For more than forty years I thought that this desire had been sweetened into love of God and Torah and disciplined into the work of service. But, returning in older age to the instincts of youth, I now entertain the thought that the desire was never lessened and the *ego cogito* never exiled. I begin to weigh a different story: in a flash, this desire may catch a glimpse of the light at its source and of its source. The glimpse may suggest that, like this photon stream in relation to that sun, this desire belongs to nothing other than God's desire and that, like this reflection of sunlight off that mirror, the "I think" serves as a potential vehicle of God's desire.

In this story, the *ego cogito* plays a rather humble role, but its desire for clarity and universal truth is no longer simply errant. It may be, within its finite location, a desire for the light and trustworthiness (troth) of God's word, by which word the whole universe is created. It may, in other words, be a desire that this finite light of reason, with its limited clarity and scope and reliability, serve as agent only of God's light and of care for God's creation. In its youth, this desire may simply have mistaken the reflected and refracted light of reason for God's light and mistaken the immediacy of reason's apparent vision for the long time it takes (a lifetime's "week" of work) to trace mirrored light back to its most proximate sources.

Textual reasoning traces one path through which the "I think" redirects itself toward its proximate sources: the finite location—of language and literature, community and service—in which God's word is received and through which our desires may serve God's. Textual reasoning is performed by way of a network of relations (social, hermeneutical, and more) that provides a place of both love and discipline for the "I think." Each individual text reading around the table shares, more or less, in the form of the "I think": the fruit of someone's judgment, at this moment, that the text displays a particular meaning. The individual is heard, but each individual must also hear the other person, and as a source of new models of judgment and not merely of new ways of testing one's own model.

The movement of textual reasoning from one reading to the next is therefore irreducible to the form of the "I think." The group's overall reasoning is not formless, but its form is enacted through its movement, and its movement passes from the fruit of one "I think" to another and another.

The form, in other words, is not of "I think" but of "we think," or (in one case) "the people Israel thinks," or "Torah is thought." This is the form we call textual reasoning. It displays itself only locally, through a given event of movement over the texts and among a given community. In this sense, textual reasoning cannot be mistaken for one instance of "universal reason"; we cannot infer from a given event of textual reasoning exactly how another event will appear, let alone how human beings do or ought to reason. At the same time, textual reasoners may receive the texts they study as displays of the Creator's word addressed—in this instance—to the people Israel. If so, textual reasoners would receive these texts as spoken by the one who also speaks to and through all creation and all humanity; this speech would therefore be a sign of God's care and instruction for all humanity, but not explicitly and not by way of any clear, distinct, and universal propositions.

Textual reasoning is a postliberal rather than strictly postmodern practice, because its critique of Enlightenment models of rationality is not a critique of Enlightenment desire for a reasoning that would instruct and mend all humanity. That desire remains, but its fulfillment is projected onto the end of days and onto a Word that speaks nonclearly or locally.

But what of scriptural reasoning? It is both like and unlike textual reasoning. It offers a play of possible readings voiced around the table, but the voices emanate from one of three different locations of language and tradition. In this sense, three text traditions seem to sit at the table, but the voices heard belong only to individuals, who speak only of scriptural texts, read apart from their commentarial traditions. A unique stream of reasoning appears gradually around the table, and once again it is irreducible to the form of "I think." But it is also irreducible to the form of "we think." Like the "I think" in textual reasoning, each traditioned "we think" is given voice but no privilege. It is invited to the feast as one guest among others. Finding no reason to resist the stream, it joins its voice to the others, but it does not know where it is being carried.

If scriptural reasoning were recommended as more than an occasional exercise, this last sentence might give me pause: too many reminders here of the Enlightenment's flight beyond language use and tradition—and I do not want to return to the childhood garden. In the words of a friend active in scriptural reasoning, Micheal O'Siadhail:

> An apple-bite and that garden vanishes
> forever. You too will roam with Adam.
> Sap in the trees' limbs still lavishes
> memories. You grow to another millennium.
> Is what we love what we find?
> Is there somewhere a second garden,
> an arbour where the quickened mind
> soars between its knowing and abandon?
> (from *The Chosen Garden*)

My change of mind is toward another enlightenment—not the one that imagined its universe within the form of "I think" and regarded untraditioned reasoning as a universal standard for everyday action in the world. In the words of Aref Nayed of Dubai, our scriptural reasoning gatherings may be brief, but the effects of scriptural reasoning are "carried in the heart." We return home to traditioned communities of belief and action. "The Lord works in the in-between (*barzakh*) that is 'triangulated' among the traditions that contribute to scriptural reasoning. This is a universalism beyond the universe and a disclosure from-above-disclosures."

The "we" of our gathering is not that of any new language community or some extralinguistic replacement. It is the we of eschatological hope, whose not-yet is not a flight from the traditioned communities but a transforming warmth that works among them through the spirit within.

Scriptural reasoning refers its vision of universal care and truth to the end of days. It offers no immediate solution to inter-Abrahamic, let alone interhuman, conflict. At the same time, it can bring the peace of the end time to one hour or three days of intimate conversation among traditional Muslims, Jews, and Christians. This practice may potentially spread to others, one table and one conversation at a time, in unpredictable ways. And in Nayed's words, the "peace of one hour or three days may enter the heart permanently."

12

Prayer as Crucible

SARAH COAKLEY

THERE IS A SENSE in which my mind has changed only once in the course of my career as a theologian, but once instigated, this change was so dramatic and transformative as to sweep everything else uncomfortably in its wake. Like a subterranean explosion, the intellectual fallout was initially difficult to trace to its source. But as I now see it, any subsequent theological changes must be seen as the direct or indirect result of this first one—and there is no end to the changes in sight.

This is not the story of a classic conversion experience, let alone of a pietistic revulsion against the intellect. On the contrary, it is an account of how prayer—especially the simple prayer of relative silence or stillness—has the power to change one's perception of the theological task. What started as an adventure in personal prayer—which drew me in much faster and more disconcertingly than I was ready for—has ended in a program for systematic theology (and its handmaid, philosophy of religion) that is as much implicated in the corporate and the social as it is in the personal. For that is where prayer inexorably leads us.

The familiar feminist slogan has a real point here: "The personal is the political." That is why what follows is by no means a narrative of individual religious experience in the modern sense analyzed most memorably by William James. Rather, it is an account of how a practice that might, at best, count as a failed Jamesian religious experience could nonetheless make a different sort of theologian out of me, one committed to what I now call theology *in via* (a theology "on the road"). And if one's theology is *in via*, then there is no horizon that does not potentially involve ever further personal change.

It has only been in the past decade that I have been fully able to see what all this might mean theologically. It is not a coincidence, I am sure, that it is also within these last ten years that I have been formed as a priest (with all the extraordinary humiliations, joys, and transformations that this necessarily involves), have fallen afoul of the secularized academic institution (Harvard Divinity School) I was trying to serve, and have struggled with a set of increasingly destructive disjunctions—both intellectual and ecclesiastical—that afflict many of us in the field of academic theology today, especially in North America. My perspective is a transatlantic one, however, for I now teach in England, and my priesthood is exercised in the university and at an English cathedral—not that many of the difficulties go away, of course.

This may so far sound like a merely personal narrative. In fact, I now realize in retrospect that the political, social, and intellectual backdrop of the time was crucial for how I responded to the initial crisis of prayer, as I shall try to indicate. But I must first attempt to speak honestly of that original subterranean explosion of prayer.

I cannot remember a time when God was not for me a holy reality and a matter of intense interest and yearning. But prayer was a problem. How on earth did one do it? Jesus gave one the simplest things to ask for (Matt 6: 9–13, etc.), but Paul seemed to admit that prayer was pretty much humanly impossible (Rom 8:26)—and that was only the first of the puzzles.

I was drawn in my childhood and adolescence to several people who had the evident aura of holiness and for whom prayer was a central focus. To find out later that their lives were, in other respects, difficult, fractured, and even morally blinkered was a paradox with which I continue to struggle. But holiness is not the same thing as psychoanalytic wholeness; and if it was prayer that made them what they were, then I wanted it too. Or rather, what I wanted was *God*.

After many attempts at daily intercession and scriptural meditation which seemed unsatisfying (although I am sure they were exactly what was needed at the time), it was in my mid-twenties that I finally found my way into a simpler form of prayer via an experiment with Transcendental Meditation. I took this up on the excuse of needing an antidote to stress in my first academic job. The impact was electrifying.

I hadn't been going longer than about two months with this simple discipline of twenty minutes of silence in the morning and early evening when what I can only call a seismic shift of seemingly unspeakable proportions began to afflict me. Whatever was going on here was not only "transcendental" but severely *real*. Clearly I was going to have to make some metaphysical choices, and fast. Either I could buy (literally) the next set of courses with the TM folk and be introduced to some important framework ideas from Vedanta, or I could seek to bring whatever was happening to me into some sort of alliance with my Christian faith. I chose the latter option.

Had movements such as centering prayer been operative at that time, my path would have been a great deal easier, and I would have known that what was happening to me was nothing special at all but part and parcel of any sustained commitment to silence. As it was, I was blundering along in the dark, and even my first attempt at seeking proper spiritual direction (which I certainly needed) ended in a painful and crushing rebuff.

Yet it was strangely impossible to step off the spiritual roller coaster which was now in full swing. I recall finding a letter of Basil the Great in which he describes the adventure of prayer as like getting into a boat with the decks constantly shifting under one; this was some comfort, as was the discovery of Bernard of Clairvaux's many meditations on the "fear of the Lord as the beginning of wisdom," fear marking the necessary cracking open of the heart before God if prayer is to develop and deepen. Since the ground was (literally and fearfully) heaving for me, too, I had urgent recourse to whatever patristic, medieval, and early modern treatises on prayer I could lay hands on. Little was I to know at the time that this was to lead me to a complete rethinking of doctrinal development in the early church and beyond.

For as I rapidly discovered, when one came at that history without the forced modern distinction between "spiritual" and "dogmatic" texts, a whole new world lay before one: spiritual growth and doctrinal truth hung newly together. The history of doctrine became likewise the entangled history of spiritual and political struggle—including intense struggles over questions of gender and authority. But this did not reduce doctrinal questions to (secularized) issues of sex and power, as was becoming a fashionable mode of analysis in the wake of Michel Foucault. On the contrary, the commitment to prayer strung one on the rack of the painful internalization of divine truth. For me, this change of approach heralded no nostalgic or romantic return to a premodern era, as was—at the other end of the spectrum from the Foucauldians—also becoming popular in various forms of neo-conservatism. Here the slogan was: "Down with the Enlightenment and back to the Fathers and medievals!" No, for me it was a retrieval of a classic tradition sweated painfully out of the exigencies of prayer encountered primarily as darkness and disturbance.

But I must not leave the impression that this adventure in prayer was all anxiety-making, although its initial impact on my sense of self as a young theologian was certainly that. Underneath was an extraordinary sense of spiritual and epistemic expansion—of being taken by the hand into a new world of glorious Technicolor, in which all one's desires were newly magnetized toward God, all beauty sharpened and intensified. Yet simultaneously all poverty, deprivation, and injustice were equally and painfully impressed with new force on my consciousness.

It was as if the darkness of fear, which had been newly hypostatized as race at the Enlightenment (perhaps because the awesome "God" in Godself was now off limits, epistemologically, according to Kant), had been firmly placed out of sight in my privileged academic education and was now hitting me from out of the depths with all the force of that which the white man cannot bear to see. This connection between Enlightenment epistemological issues and the modern question of race really became clear to me only when I was doing prison chaplaincy work in a jail in Boston during my priestly formation. (See my article "Jail Break: Meditation as Subversive Activity," *Christian Century*, June 29, 2004.)

I was myself now on the margins, seeing things all aslant. I was forced to reconsider the very nature of the human intellect, its goals and its tasks, its relations to affect and especially to what the Christian tradition has called spiritual sensation.

Lest this seem like a claim to some special supernatural encounter, I hasten to add that the daily practice of silence itself was usually more like the tedious quotidian discipline of brushing one's teeth than anything else. It was the effects outside prayer—including, of course, the effects on other normal Christian or academic duties (hearing the Word, participating in the sacraments, attending to students in difficulties, writing lectures, and so on)—that were initially hard to quantify and yet palpably transforming of all my previous theological assumptions.

I had been trained at Cambridge in an era of benign but somewhat vapid biblical liberalism, which irritated me not because it was liberal (that was more the complaint of my fellow student Rowan Williams, I think) but because for the most part it failed to probe the philosophical assumptions it was making about the relation between scriptural texts, historical verifiability, and theological truth. Propelled by these historiographical concerns, I followed up my initial degree, after a brief spell at Harvard, with a dissertation focused on Ernst Troeltsch's Christology. ("You could write *that* on a postage stamp," remarked Stephen Sykes, my Cambridge teacher in systematics; I set out with the arrogance of youth to prove him wrong.) I was driven by a desire to pinpoint the precise philosophical conditions under which incarnational claims for Christ would seem probative; my mind-set—more unconscious than conscious, I suspect—was that of classic British foundationalism (the philosophical doctrine that says all legitimate claims to truth must be "founded" in certain basic, unassailable truths which all thinking subjects have in common—e.g., those which are known directly by the senses or are self-evident or logically irrefutable). I must have imbibed Locke with my mother's milk, for at Cambridge I mainly read Hume and Kant (under the eccentric tutelage of Donald MacKinnon), followed by my beloved Troeltsch, whom I sought to reinstate after Barth's savage critique.

Round about the time I was finishing the doctoral thesis, however, the bottom fell out of those fundamental philosophical assumptions which I had simply taken for granted. What I had thought were just some nasty bumps in the area of my spiritual life was impinging with force on my entire philosophical agenda.

It took me many years to bring these changes in my theological picture to full fruition and to have the courage to express them explicitly and boldly. But in recent years I can say that this has at last happened, urged on by the necessary integration of pastoral and theological tasks occasioned by my ordination process.

Three particular shifts can perhaps form my focus in this article. Of course, they did not occur without impact from the surrounding intellectual and political circumstances of North America in the same decade, as I shall try to clarify. One might say that they arose in a sort of tense contrapuntal relation to the new theological disjunctions of the time, both liberal and conservative. But they seemingly fitted neither of these parties with any ease.

Control and loss of control: Powers and submissions. At the heart of the prayer of silence is a simple surrendering of control to God. Instead of a busy setting of one's own agendas, prayer becomes pared down to wanting

God alone—"with the sharp darts of longing love," as the author of *The Cloud of Unknowing* memorably puts it. This is not to say that petition or intercession are abandoned—far from it. But they are now set in the context of an underlying submission to the divine: as Paul has it, this ceding of place is to the Spirit, who prays in us and for us (and others), with sighs too deep for words.

The discipline of learning this particular submission to the unique source of one's being is initially disturbing and even weird, especially for anyone who has been trained to master material and to put her chosen mark on it. "The intellect faces a blank and the will follows it," as Dom John Chapman aptly described this curious way of "wasting time" before God. But then should one not expect an intentional noetic interaction with God to be unlike any other interaction? Should one be surprised if the effect is dizzying? It took me a long while to come to terms with this fundamental problem and its implications.

Not only was this shift into practiced loss of control intrinsically anxiety-making, it also brought with it for me a taxing feminist paradox. Was not lack of control, lack of autonomy, precisely the problem that women were countering with feminism? Was not vulnerability an ill to be avoided rather than a precious state to be inculcated? Was not this, in other words, a dangerous invitation to sexist discrimination, even abuse? (I recall Elisabeth Schüssler Fiorenza, at the time of my appointment to Harvard in 1991, insisting that I stop talking and writing about vulnerability.)

It took me a while to work out that a seriously false dichotomy was at work here, and that submission to God and silence before God—being unlike any other submission or any other silence—was that which empowered one to speak against injustice and abuse and was the ground of true freedom (in God) rather than its suppression. (Of course, this set me against much American liberal feminism and womanism of the time, to my distress.)

It also took patience to grasp—through the deeper engagement with scripture and tradition that this practice was also drawing me into—that my whole concept of the bounds of selfhood was undergoing change. The meaning of the "body of Christ" in Paul sprang alive for the first time and with that a mysterious sense of our deep mutual implication in each other's lives as members of that body. And if this was what Christ meant for the here and now, then surely it must signal that my previous assumptions about a past, extrinsic "life of Jesus" as the only basis for Christology was wildly awry and fatally restricted (sorry, Troeltsch). The resurrection had reappeared—reentering triumphantly by stealth through the back door of my consciousness. Moreover, what had started as a frighteningly lonely journey of prayer now seemed to be the least lonely activity that one could possibly engage in—not only buzzing with communication, but positively crowded with angels and saints, the living and the dead.

Sex, bodiliness, and the mystery of desire. This brings me to my second point of dramatic change. No less disturbing than the loss of noetic control in prayer and all that followed from that was the arousal, intensification, and reordering of desire that this praying engendered. Anyone who has spent more than a short time on her or his knees in silence will know of the almost farcical raid that the unconscious makes on us in the sexual arena in such prayer, as if this is a sort of joke that God has up God's sleeve to ensure that ourselves, our souls, and bodies are what we present to God and not some pious disembodied version of such. Our capacity as Christians to try to keep sex and God in different boxes is seemingly limitless, but the integrative force of silent prayer simply will not allow this, or not for very long.

Huge difficulties need to be confronted here, and I do not think they can be faced quickly or without real pain and danger. Moreover, trying to make sense of all this in the face of currently fashionable postmodern gender theory has created some real points of contact in my recent theology, but also revealed deep differences in fundamental approach.

What is at stake from my perspective is not so much the overturning of societal gender stereotypes à la philosopher Judith Butler (though the courage engendered by prayer tends to lead there quite naturally) but rather the urgent question of how all our desires—not just for sex, but for money, power, fame, and immortality—may be thrown by prayer into the purifying crucible of divine desire. There is our own primary desire for God, of course, which we strive in prayer to put first; but underlying that is God's unique and unchangeable desire for us, without which all our own striving is fruitless. As John of the Cross acknowledges so wonderfully in "The Living Flame," at the end of his own long journey of desire: once all our desires are sorted and purged (not, note, repressed or obliterated) we enter a realm of infinite delight-in-God.

In other words, what prayer teaches, but only painfully and over time, is the ascetical task of acknowledging—and then adjudicating between—competing desires jostling within us, both good and ill. The acid test is the conformity to divine will (a matter on which we are often not best able to judge for ourselves—confession, direction, and the help of our friends-in-Christ is crucial). But torn as we are now between the false modern alternatives of liberal libertinism and conservative repression, this precious third, ascetical alternative is seemingly a lost art in the affluent world of the West. The trouble is, it cannot in any case be our art to own and control: there is no escaping the hard graft of painful self-knowledge, patience—and prayer. God does the work in us if we allow it.

When future historians look back at this extraordinary period of ecclesiastical schisms over sex and gender, it will perhaps be possible to see this set of ructions not as the last prurient gasp of reactionary forces but as a more general crisis of what may be called the economy of desire. An erotic maturity is palpably lacking in our supposedly civilized world, and it cannot be commodified or hastened. It is an ascetic task for each one of us. While liberals say that we should stop worrying about sexual continence and start feeding the poor or saving the planet, conservatives rejoin that the whole planet is cosmically disordered in the first place if sexual desire is out of place. What if, again, both these alternatives are false ones, and sexual desire has to be dealt with alongside all these other desires, so that their "orientation" is finally ordered to God? On such a view, the wholly modern (intrinsically secular?) categorization of hetero-, homo-, and bisexuality might fall into the background as distractions from this more urgent task. Any quest for integrity, truth, and honesty will be suppressed here at self-defeating cost.

Rationality and its expansion: Variations on post-foundationalism. The third area in which my mind has been changed is importantly related to the first two, but takes me into the realm of philosophy of religion, in which field my current post at Cambridge is focused. In a period when there has been a remarkable set of attacks on classical foundationalism by both philosophers and theologians, I have again felt myself to be plowing a subtly different course as a result of the prayer perspective I have tried to outline above. For the danger of the various theological critiques of such foundationalism (whether Thomist, Calvinist, Wittgensteinian, or Barthian in inspiration) is that they can jump on a current secular philosophical bandwagon—the fashionable raging against the Enlightenment—without supplying any very effective account of how theology can continue to engage philosophically with secular thought and still truly challenge it. Rhetorical fiat alone will not do the trick. For theologies in this environment all too easily become a series of loudly announced but basically unargued sectarian assertions. This is the "anarchy of values" of which Wilhelm Dilthey so presciently spoke and with which philosophers such as John McIntyre and Charles Taylor (and, in his different way, Alvin Plantinga) have struggled afresh of late with great sophistication.

My own response to this philosophical and theological crisis is one that seeks to analyze the dark testing of contemplation as precisely an epistemological challenge. In other words, I continue to reject another false modern disjunction—that between spirituality and philosophy. It is not that contemplation affords just another sectarian theological perspective, which one can take or leave as one wills. Rather, its painful and often dark expansion of consciousness, its integration of thought and affect, and its ethical sensitizing to what is otherwise neglected (including, of course, the poor "who are always with us") all demand that one give an account of how philosophy—and science and politics, too—cannot ultimately afford to ignore the apprehensions that contemplation invites.

Clearly this is a hugely ambitious philosophical program, and one that I am only now beginning to work out. The move from old-style rational proofs for God's existence to dark, contemplative testing is emphatically not just a matter of adding prayer experience and stirring. There is an expansion of reason's remit here, a reconsideration of the place of affect, of epistemic training, and of responsive integration (with interesting points of contact with the best recent turns in feminist epistemology), and an acknowledgment of the powerful ways in which what we prefer not to see dangerously affects what we *can* see. This has implications well beyond the theological camp: science itself is not immune. You could call this project a form of nonfoundationalism, but not quite of the usual sort. This is where my thought is heading in the coming years—if life and energy endure.

I have attempted to explain how a practice which I first took up as a young theologian in my early twenties has disconcertingly changed my mind about almost everything—God, theology, philosophy, politics, race, and feminism—and in ways I could scarcely even have imagined at the outset of the adventure. But particularly in the past decade, and against the backdrop of increasingly sharp tensions between postliberal, neoconservative, and late-liberal schools of theology, I have come to see what it all might mean for me as a theologian and a priest. As the ecclesiastical world fractures over sex, and the academic world drives an increasingly false wedge between the study of religion and Christian theology, I find myself deeply uneasy with these particular battles and their presumptions. Yet, as I have been writing this essay (a task not itself without its own pain and difficulty),

I have become freshly aware how obvious it was that I could be nothing but an irritant to the new regime of mandatory secularism (in the name of the academic study of religion) that came in at Harvard under President Larry Summers and has continued on today. The students themselves were perplexed by these disjunctions, of course; many of them had come to Harvard, after all, precisely to train as scholar-ministers and to integrate a calling to the church with the highest endeavors in theological learning.

In the coming decade we may perhaps hope to see some resolution of these current theological impasses. I am full of such hope. In the meantime I can only rejoice that Cambridge has welcomed me home and provided the ideal environment for me to continue having my mind changed. I have to say that I do not find the ground any firmer than it ever was in this strange, enticing journey into God.

13

Global Engagement

MAX L. STACKHOUSE

MY MATERNAL GRANDFATHER, M. B. Graham, was an evangelical Methodist preacher who for a time was assigned to a congregation in northern Indiana. A leader in that congregation was James Stackhouse. His son, Dale—my father—won scholarships to DePauw University and Boston University School of Theology and ended up being a minister and marrying the preacher's youngest daughter. So my nurture into Methodist piety, conservative and liberal, was charted from the start.

It was a loving, pious environment in which to grow up. My preacher grandfather built me a pulpit when I was three and encouraged me to preach (from the Methodist Hymnal; I was not qualified to preach from the Bible). My grandfather and father would debate my message, while the whole family loved singing whatever hymns I chose.

In junior high school a teacher asked us to write papers on possible vocations. My first pick was easy: minister. At summer church camp, along with playing sports, we had classes in Bible, missions, and beliefs. The camp ended with decision night, where we had to decide what we were going to do with our lives. I gave my life to Christ on one such night, figuring that being a Supreme Court judge or a forest ranger could be considered a social ministry if church work didn't pan out. It was a very emotional time. It was also the week that I first kissed a girl.

As a "pre-theo" major at DePauw University I joined the Philosophy Club, which met in the home of Professor Warren Steinkraus. The group talked of Plato and Aristotle, Kant and Hegel, Locke and Marx—but also of Senator Joe McCarthy, who was accusing people of being un-American. Steinkraus was devoted to personal idealism and Methodism, which he took in a radical direction. As a pacifist, socialist, and advocate of integration, he railed against McCarthy. After I saw McCarthy in action on TV, I soon became anti-McCarthy too.

Another Methodist philosopher at DePauw was Russell Compton, who was fascinated by phenomenology, process thought, and existentialism as well as by social questions. Together these professors posed questions that have troubled me ever since.

I was a very uncomfortable Methodist in those days, but I still accepted an assignment by the bishop to be a student supply pastor at a tiny Methodist church in a played-out strip mining village nearby. I was reading books by the Quaker theologian Elton Trueblood as well as Marx, Camus, and Sartre. I was a pacifist, socialist, agnostic "radical." My sermons must have puzzled my little flock. But they adopted me anyway.

This period reflected my first conscious change of mind. On campus, I joined the left-leaning Jefferson-Jackson Club, led by Vernon Jordan (who later became an adviser to President Clinton). We had fourteen members, whereas the Young Republicans had several hundred (this was Indiana, after all). I began writing a column for the campus newspaper called "The Ax by Max."

What to do after college? Despite decision night, I had no clarity on this score. A professor told me about a scholarship being offered by the Netherlands for Americans to study at the new Institute for Foreign Service and International Trade (now Nijenrode Business University). The Netherlands was grateful for postwar support from the United States, and it wanted to cement relations with the United States and acquaint future Dutch leaders with potential leaders from abroad. I filled out the form the professor conveniently presented. That's how in 1957 I found myself on a ship to Rotterdam, headed for Nijenrode.

Besides intensively studying Dutch, I was introduced at Nijenrode to economics and the "science of management," to European political history and the arts of diplomacy, and to what it means to live in a multicultural world. Three particular experiences there shaped my later thinking.

First, when the English instructor became ill and I was asked to fill in, I discovered that I loved teaching. I began to consider teaching as a vocation.

Second, for my independent study project, I chose to work on Martin Heidegger, whom I understood to be the most radical thinker of the times. After reading chunks of his work I concluded that he had nothing to offer on the social questions that were troubling me and that he had no rock on which to stand to support what he did think. When I found out that he had been a Nazi during World War II, I completely lost interest in his thought and its existentialist and postmodern heirs.

My adviser told me about one thinker who was influenced by existentialism but took it in a different direction—Paul Tillich, then at Harvard. "Besides," he said, "you are not only interested in social issues, you are obsessed with religion. You should go there."

Third, I was introduced to the thought of Abraham Kuyper, the Calvinist theologian who was also the founder of the Free University in Amsterdam and who served as prime minister of Holland earlier in the century.

Theology, higher education, and public service. Was I being guided in some way?

I went to Harvard Divinity School to study with Tillich. I found many other intellectual stars in their own orbits there. Tillich and Erik Erikson were the best lecturers. Tillich argued that faith included and comprehended doubt and that doubt was necessary, for it forced one to be honest about the faith—a message I was relieved to hear. Erikson pointed out that biography influenced faith, which I already knew, but also that faith influenced the stances that people and societies take, as he had documented in his books on Luther and Gandhi—a message I wanted to find out more about.

In spite of his turgid style, the sociologist Talcott Parsons convinced me that most social changes are made through the interactions of multiple social systems in which religion is a key factor. Reinhold Niebuhr was a visiting professor in those years, and both his break with pacifism and his understanding of human nature confirmed my critical evaluation of the easy conscience of contemporary idealism.

Yet in this period Martin Luther King Jr. was leading the nonviolent boycotts and marches that were to change American life. It is hard to overestimate the impact that King had on theologians and seminarians of my generation. He opened the door to a new role for pastors: shaping society's awareness of justice issues. I became deeply involved in the civil rights movement. I marched at Selma, organized teach-ins, and lectured at innumerable adult educational events in church basements. My wife and I joined a black United Church of Christ congregation in Boston.

Throughout this time, my primary mentor was James Luther Adams, a self-professed Christian Unitarian-Universalist. His account of the Puritan legacy and of thinkers such as Walter Rauschenbusch, Max Weber, and Ernst Troeltsch convinced me that it is possible to be a believer, to be constructively pertinent to society, and to be intellectually critical. He also helped me see the importance of voluntary associations (of which the church is the historical model) and of the right to freely organize them. His emphasis on forming a public ethos that could evoke responsible participation in covenanted relationships seemed to me both inspiring and practical. I became convinced that a Reformed theological framework was faithful to the biblical heritage and that it could support the social changes I thought needed to happen better than any other worldview I had encountered.

I was ordained in the UCC and served as assistant pastor in Lincoln, Massachusetts, before being appointed to teach social ethics at Andover Newton Theological School. I loved the work with seminarians. I challenged and nurtured them as best I could, continually drawing on lessons gleaned from my family, DePauw, Nijenrode, and Harvard.

Two developments in these years further changed my perspectives. One was a cooperative arrangement that began between Andover Newton and the theology department of Boston College. The Second Vatican Council had occurred, and many had hopes that an ecumenical spirit would lead to new relations between Catholics and Protestants. The faculties of Andover Newton and Boston College formed a joint graduate program designed to foster dialogue and learning. We began fertile exchanges in all the major fields.

The Vietnam War was forcing Protestant ethicists to consider Catholic teachings about just and unjust wars. A modified version of just war doctrine became so convincing to me that I began to consider pacifism to be an immoral posture of self-righteousness, a way of saying: "I (or we) are faithful and good because we do no harm; but you (or they) are unfaithful and evil because of the use of coercive power to try to establish the relatively just peace possible in human affairs." This stance not only ignores the multiple kinds and levels of coercive force that exist (as Niebuhr had recognized) but fails to recognize that sometimes the only way to approximate a just peace is to control evil by force of arms and that some people may have a genuine calling to serve in the military, police, or security forces.

Though learning from Catholics about the just war tradition, I thought Catholics were mistaken on several aspects of sexual and family ethics. Nonetheless, I thought they were correct in principle when they argued that homosexuality is "objectively disordered" according to the best standards one could derive from scripture, tradition, and reasoned reflection on God-given natural law. I have come to regret taking that view, though I do not think it can be dismissed as simply based in hate or homophobia. I do think that it must be modulated by the recognition that scripture, tradition, and natural law also provide the strongest bases for affirming that all persons are created in the image of God and that we should affirm the dignity and civil rights of each person.

The second set of events that changed my outlook in these years was ecumenical contacts of another kind. The Mission Board of the United Church of Christ asked me to work as a consultant, and this led me first to work with sister churches in South Africa in fighting apartheid and then, in 1973, to teach at the United Theological College in Bangalore, India, a training ground for pastors in the United Church of South India.

My wife and I packed up our three children and boarded a plane bound for Bombay. We learned in time to cope with the routine complexities of living in India and grew to treasure that country and the people we met. India was and is a fascinatingly rich compound of clashing cultural and social dynamics. There is great wealth for some, crushing poverty for many, magnificent beauty and woeful ugliness, ancient tradition and rapid modernization—distributed among a variety of tribal, Hindu, Muslim, Buddhist, Marxist, peasant, and urbanite peoples and overlaid with a passion for the democratic socialist legacy that Gandhi, Nehru, and the Congress Party had adapted from the British Laborites. Unfortunately, the nation had also borrowed from the Raj bureaucratic forms of administration, which were quickly fitted out with the indigenous and pervasive caste system. Caste dominated even in Christian communities, though they fought against it.

All in all, India was a veritable living museum of social arrangements and religiously sanctioned social ethics, the whole swimming in spirituality. As chaotic as it sometimes seemed, it also bore the deep marks of a long history and a great civilization stamped by the Hindu metaphysical vision—obviously one of the major options for forming a social order.

Many Indians tended to blame Western capitalism and colonialism for their poverty, but a few were asking how to create an ethos that could overcome poverty and make human rights real. That triggered questions which I began to research and discuss in the classroom: What forms an ethos in the first place? What can induce changes in a traditional ethos? Given the fact that biologically and in terms of material needs people are pretty much the same everywhere, what makes the difference between an ethos that fosters economic development, a democratic civil society, and respect for human rights and one that inhibits these institutions? It is not only economic interests and forces at work, I argued. What then does the church have to offer in the name of Christ?

In the mid-1970s I found myself drawn into a debate about the relationship of Christianity to Western culture. In 1973, a group of evangelical leaders were called together by Richard Mouw and John Howard Yoder to issue the Chicago Declaration, a profession of their faith in Jesus and a confession of the complicity of evangelicals in the injustices and infidelities of American culture. This declaration was one of the earliest clarion calls for evangelicals to enter political debates—a movement that had enormous effect over the next several decades.

A year later, another group of theologians were called together by Lutheran pastor Richard John Neuhaus and sociologist Peter Berger. This group issued the Hartford Appeal, which lamented the way modern thought had lost a sense of transcendence. The cause of this loss was the heretical beliefs that modern thought is superior to past forms of understanding reality, that religious thought is independent of rational discourse, and that religious language refers only to human experience, God being humanity's invention. The Hartford group attacked the idea that all religions are equal and a matter of personal preference and that being true to oneself is the meaning of salvation. The statement was a sharp polemic against Christian leaders who focus on social ills or contemporary social issues rather than on the doctrines and dogmas of the faith.

At the time, I was on the board of the Boston Industrial Mission. Norman Faramelli of the Mission called together the board and friends, including Harvard theologian Harvey Cox, to study these two documents. We debated over several evenings and found that there were aspects of both statements that we could affirm. But we thought neither of the documents offered a strong sense that the God of the Bible has much to do with social, cultural, or intellectual matters except to condemn them—one in the name of loving and obeying Jesus, the other in defense of the creedal traditions. One document smacked of Billy Graham and the search for what could save us from the pending doom of a culture gone wrong, the other of Karl Barth and the call for a return to church dogmatics.

Our group had no doubt that there was injustice in the world that needed prophetic critique, but none of us believed that a blanket condemnation of modern civilization was warranted, or that believing Christians could or should live entirely outside of or against culture. The question was what resources the church had to confront the evils and superficial ideologies that obscured the faith's partial incarnation in modern society.

Our response to Chicago and Hartford, titled the Boston Affirmations, was intended to be a biblically based theological warrant for ecumenical Christians to selectively engage in and defend aspects of modern culture while participating in the critical examination of it in conversation with popular culture, philosophy, the social sciences, and various struggles for justice. Although there was vigorous debate within our group on just about every point, we finally came to a general consensus. I was elected as scribe and wrote the final draft. These themes have shaped my work since, although now looking back on these debates I realize that I and others from Boston drew more on themes from evangelical and classical sources than we may have realized—and more than the Chicago or Hartford groups may have realized in the ferment of the culture wars that followed in the next decades.

Connections with the UCC's Mission Board led me in the late 1970s to a series of consultations in the German Democratic Republic on theological education in a socialist environment. UCC leaders wondered what the U.S. church could learn from and offer to GDR Christians. With the cold war at a peak, we sought to develop a *Kirchengemeinschaft* (church communion) with Christians behind the iron curtain. In fact, I was invited to be a visiting professor there for a term. By this time I had joined the religious caucus of the Democratic Socialist Organizing Committee, which operated on the left wing of the Democratic Party. I was interested in the prospects for a Christian democratic socialism that could help reconcile East and West.

My East German theology students met me with a polite but solid wall of resistance. They agreed that Christianity could become democratic in principle—since the church as they knew it contained the promise of democratic practices, even if it was not democratic at the moment. But they insisted that socialism as they lived in it and had been taught it at school, in youth organizations, and by the state-controlled media could become neither Christianized nor democratized (in the sense of having plural parties and voluntary groups with civil liberties under constitutional law); socialism was a totalizing system. They disagreed with church leaders who thought that Christianity could reform and humanize East bloc socialism.

The students chided me for not understanding what "really existing socialism" meant in terms of restrictions on church life, family life, educational opportunity, employment, labor unions, ecology, and the arts. You have to decide, they said in a fatherly tone: "If Christianity is your criterion for choosing, do you choose democracy or socialism? You can't sit on the wall!" (Some ten students in that seminar would later participate in the candlelight demonstrations at a church in Leipzig in 1989 that led to the fall of the Berlin Wall, and several were elected to a provisional governing body during the transition to a united Germany.)

When I returned home, I reported my experiences to the religious caucus of the Democratic Socialist Organizing Committee. "Well," asked one fellow theologian, "what did you decide?" I said, "If it comes to a choice, it would be democracy." He replied, "Wrong choice!"

My choice alienated me from some of my former teachers and most of the caucus members. That experience converted me away from socialism and plunged me deeper into the study of economics. I began to read more deeply about the history of Christian ethical teachings on business, the independent (non-state-run) corporation and the relation of religion to economic life—topics little understood in most seminaries.

Following a move from Andover Newton to a post on the faculty of Princeton Theological Seminary, another international horizon opened up. I was invited to join the board of the China Academic Consortium, which is dedicated to cultivating dialogue between Western Christian philosophers, theologians, and ethicists and Chinese academics in related fields. It was at about this time that the Chinese Communist Party made the decision to shift to a social market economy and began its striking move toward allowing a limited form of capitalism.

Some Chinese intellectuals were beginning to turn from Karl Marx to Max Weber and to consider whether the West is wealthy and powerful because of the influence of Christianity. They wanted to know whether this was true and what the connection is between religion and social ethics. Many of them had lost confidence in Confucian and Maoist values. Over the next several years, I attended seven consultations in China and had a chance to visit many parts of the country—all of which were undergoing rapid social change. I attended both state-approved churches and independent ones.

But the core of my work had to do with scholars interested in the ways in which major Christian motifs shaped the ethos that generated democracy, human rights, corporate capitalism, and modern technology and thereby the forces behind globalization—something they energetically favor. These thinkers are commonly called "cultural Christians" in the Chinese context, and their influence is growing among Chinese intellectuals and, some say, in the Communist Party. I was drawn into consultations with graduate students and their professors who were preparing theses (mostly in literature, the social sciences, history, or philosophy) that treat religion as a basic, if sometimes indirect, sociocultural cause—a view of religion officially frowned upon by the government. A number were interested in the Kuyper Center for Public Theology founded at Princeton Seminary in these years.

On the basis of the exposures I have partially reviewed here, I was asked to organize two projects sponsored by the Center of Theological Inquiry at Princeton. One is a series of volumes on theological ethics and the spheres of life under the general title God and Globalization, with contributions from leading Western thinkers and a few from Asia and Africa. The other is a pair of volumes published in India seeking to redefine missions in view of the concerns of social ethics and new global developments. It is titled News of Boundless Riches, with contributions mostly from Asian scholars and some from the West.

Now that I am retired from teaching, my involvement with these topics is less through direct engagement with students than through books and articles written over the years. I cannot end this excursion into how my mind has changed without offering a word of gratitude to my forebears, teachers, colleagues, and leaders of the various institutions who drew me into successive opportunities that brought revisions of mind. They and my family have led this Indiana preacher's kid to hopes for an eventual inclusive, cosmopolitan, global civilization touched by Christ's Spirit.

Contributors

Scott Cairns is the author of six books of poetry, including *Recovered Body* and *Compass of Affection*. He's written a spiritual memoir, *Short Trip to the Edge*; a book of adaptations and translations of the work of Christian mystics, *Love's Immensity*; and, most recently, *The End of Suffering*. He teaches at the University of Missouri.

Sarah Coakley taught at Harvard Divinity School and is now professor of divinity at the University of Cambridge. She is a priest in the Church of England. Her books include *Powers and Submissions: Spirituality, Philosophy, and Gender*. She is working on a four-volume systematic theology, the first volume of which is *God, Sexuality and the Self: An Essay "On the Trinity."*

David F. Ford is professor of divinity at the University of Cambridge. His books include *Self and Salvation; Scripture and Theology: Reading Texts, Seeking Wisdom*; and the widely read textbook *The Modern Theologians: An Introduction to 20th Century Theology*.

Paul J. Griffiths teaches at Duke Divinity School. His books include *Christianity Through Non-Christian Eyes; Lying: An Augustinian Theology of Duplicity*; and *Intellectual Appetite: A Theological Grammar*.

Douglas John Hall is professor emeritus of theology at McGill University in Montreal. His books include *God and Human Suffering; The Cross in Context*; and *Confessing the Faith: Christian Theology in a North American Context*.

David Heim has been executive editor of the *Christian Century*, a biweekly magazine of religion, politics, and culture, since 1998. He has written hundreds of signed and unsigned articles for the magazine, as well as reviews for the *Washington Post* and other journals.

Robert W. Jenson taught at Lutheran Theological Seminary at Gettysburg and has been a senior scholar at the Center for Theological Inquiry at Princeton. His books include *Systematic Theology* (2 vols.); *On Thinking the Human*; a commentary on Song of Songs (for the Interpretation series); and a commentary on Ezekiel (for the Brazos Theological Commentary series).

Mark Noll teaches church history at the University of Notre Dame. His books include *The Scandal of the Evangelical Mind*; *The Civil War as a Theological Crisis*; and *The New Shape of World Christianity: How American Experience Reflects Global Faith*.

Peter Ochs teaches at the University of Virginia. His books include *Another Reformation: Postliberal Christianity and the Jews* and *Textual Reasonings: Jewish Philosophy and Text Study at the End of the Twentieth Century* (edited with Nancy Levene).

Max L. Stackhouse recently wrote *Globalization and Grace*, volume four in the God and Globalization series. He taught at Princeton Theological Seminary. His other books include *Covenant and Commitments: Faith, Family and Economic Life* and *Creeds, Society and Human Rights: A Study in Three Cultures*.

Kathryn Tanner teaches at Yale Divinity School and previously taught at the University of Chicago Divinity School. Her writings include *Christ the Key*; *Economy of Grace*; and *Jesus, Humanity, and the Trinity*

Emilie M. Townes teaches at Yale Divinity School. She is the author of *Breaking the Fine Rain of Death: African American Health and a Womanist Ethic of Care* and *Womanist Ethics and the Cultural Production of Evil*.

Nicholas Wolterstorff is professor emeritus of philosophical theology at Yale. His books include *Divine Discourse: Philosophical Reflections on the Claim That God Speaks*; *Justice: Rights and Wrongs*; and *Justice in Love*.

Carol Zaleski, professor of world religions at Smith College, is the author of *Otherworld Journeys: Accounts of Near-Death Experience in Medieval and Modern Times* and *The Life of the World to Come.* She is co-author (with Philip Zaleski) of *Prayer: A History* and *The Book of Heaven.*